CRITICAL ESSAYS O

THE CENTRAL

TO

03.

CANTERBURY TALES

Geoffrey Chaucer

Longman Literature Guides

Editors: Linda Cookson and Bryan Loughrey

Titles in the series:

CONTENTS

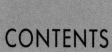

PREFACE

Like all professional groups, literary critics have developed their own specialised language. This is not necessarily a bad thing. Sometimes complex concepts can only be described in a terminology far removed from everyday speech. Academic jargon, however, creates an unnecessary barrier between the critic and the intelligent but less practised reader.

This danger is particularly acute where scholarly books and articles are re-packaged for a student audience. Critical anthologies, for example, often contain extracts from longer studies originally written for specialists. Deprived of their original context, these passages can puzzle and at times mislead. The essays in this volume, however, are all specially commissioned, self-contained works, written with the needs of students firmly in mind.

This is not to say that the contributors — all experienced critics and teachers — have in any way attempted to simplify the complexity of the issues with which they deal. On the contrary, they explore the central problems of the text from a variety of critical perspectives, reaching conclusions which are challenging and at times mutually contradictory.

They try, however, to present their arguments in direct, accessible language and to work within the limitations of scope and length which students inevitably face. For this reason, essays are generally rather briefer than is the practice; they address quite specific topics; and, in line with examination requirements, they incorporate precise textual detail into the body of the discussion.

They offer, therefore, working examples of the kind of essay-writing skills which students themselves are expected to develop. Their diversity, however, should act as a reminder that in the field of literary studies there is no such thing as a 'model' answer. Good essays are the outcome of a creative engagement with literature, of sensitive, attentive reading and careful thought. We hope that those contained in this volume will encourage students to return to the most important starting point of all, the text itself, with renewed excitement and the determination to explore more fully their own critical responses.

How to use this volume

Obviously enough, you should start by reading the text in question. The one assumption that all the contributors make is that you are already familiar with this. It would be helpful, of course, to have read further — perhaps other works by the same author or by influential contemporaries. But we don't assume that you have yet had the opportunity to do this and any references to historical background or to other works of literature are explained.

You should, perhaps, have a few things to hand. It is always a good idea to keep a copy of the text nearby when reading critical studies. You will almost certainly want to consult it when checking the context of quotations or pausing to consider the validity of the critic's interpretation. You should also try to have access to a good dictionary, and ideally a copy of a dictionary of literary terms as well. The contributors have tried to avoid jargon and to express themselves clearly and directly. But inevitably there will be occasional words or phrases with which you are unfamiliar. Finally, we would encourage you to make notes, summarising not just the argument of each essay but also your own responses to what you have read. So keep a pencil and notebook at the ready.

Suitably equipped, the best thing to do is simply begin with whichever topic most interests you. We have deliberately organised each volume so that the essays may be read in any order. One consequence of this is that, for the sake of clarity and self-containment, there is occasionally a degree of overlap between essays. But at least you are not forced to follow one — fairly arbitrary — reading sequence.

Each essay is followed by brief 'Afterthoughts', designed to highlight points of critical interest. But remember, these are only there to remind you that it is *your* responsibility to question what you read. The essays printed here are not a series of 'model' answers to be slavishly imitated and in no way should they be regarded as anything other than a guide or stimulus for your own thinking. We hope for a critically involved response: 'That was interesting. But if *I* were tackling the topic . . .!'

Read the essays in this spirit and you'll pick up many of the skills of critical composition in the process. We have, however, tried to provide more explicit advice in 'A practical guide to essay writing'. You may find this helpful, but do not imagine it offers any magic formulas. The quality of your essays ultimately depends on the quality of your engagement with literary texts. We hope this volume spurs you on to read these with greater understanding and to explore your responses in greater depth.

A note on the text

All references are to *The Riverside Chaucer* (Oxford, 1988).

Paul Norgate

*Paul Norgate teaches English at
Wavesey Hills School and has published
widely in the field of literary criticism.*

ESSAY

'A compaignye of sondry folk': the structure of Chaucer's *General Prologue*

In that endlessly fascinating activity, observing and criticising
our fellow human beings, we are mainly accustomed to describe
and judge people by reference to their involvement in action and
events. In much critical discussion of literature, this inter-
relation has been paralleled and formalised, so that 'character'
is seen to shape 'plot' as 'plot' defines 'character'. Chaucer's
General Prologue to *The Canterbury Tales* of course contains
plenty of 'character': from the Knight with his roll-call of
campaigns to the Merchant and his insolvency, from the Wife
of Bath 'wandrynge by the weye' to the Reeve who rides 'the
hyndreste of oure route' — there are sufficient characters here
to cast a blockbuster novel plus a soap opera or two (and hints
of sufficient scandal to keep the tabloid press busy for several
days). But there is little 'plot', in the sense of a continuous
storyline; so what holds together this sequence of vividly indi-
vidualised portraits?

The opening section of the *General Prologue* — the way in
which the text sets itself up to present the sequence of portraits

— provides some clues to the pattern and structure of the poem. There is the rapid sketching in of a season, an occasion and a location, and within forty or so lines our narrator has begun to circulate around the bar of the Tabard Inn, describing the characters he meets. Narrative is kept to a minimum, and most readers will probably conclude that the main function of these lines is in some way symbolic. In the 'compaignye of sondry folk' who gather in springtime to become a 'felaweship' (ll.24–26), we might detect a developing dream of ideal harmony; a faith that all men can be led to God; a belief that heterogeneous individuals can be integrated into a cohesive society, with the instant acceptance of our narrator into the community of strangers providing an appropriately symbolic conclusion to this opening section of the poem. These, after all, are fairly conventional notions of desired and desirable states, spiritual and secular, which have exerted great power and influence not only in the age of Chaucer.

Closer reading, however, indicates that, rather than conventional symbolism, what is going on in these opening lines of the *General Prologue* is actually some subtle re-arrangement of conventional expectations. Where we might, for instance, have assumed pilgrimage to be a single-mindedly spiritual enterprise — 'the hooly blisful martir for to seke' (l.17) — straightaway in this poem we are asked to comprehend a whole variety of impulses and energies which may prompt people to go off on a pilgrimage. Along with the seasonal rhythms of the natural world, elements of (at the least) instinct, circumstance and curiosity are all recognised to be at work as well as conventional piety. Within the poetic rhythms of the opening sentence of Chaucer's text ('Whan . . . And . . .; Whan . . . And . . .; Thanne . . . And . . . And . . .') these disparate motives are seen to mix, accumulate and co-exist; riding, as it were, side by side.

Pilgrimage is of course always symbolic as well as literal; not merely a journey to an actual place, but also a metaphor enacting an inner journey (that of the soul towards God). The *General Prologue* will make use of both literal and symbolic dimensions. Literal, since the act of pilgrimage occasions (and so enables in the poem) a coming-together of characters and types from across the whole spectrum of society. Symbolic, since for the society within which the *General Prologue* was written, and which formed its original audience, pilgrimage was a significant means of endorsing publicly the beliefs and values which that society took as central to its own existence. Pilgrimage, we might say then, provides in the *Prologue* a metaphor for a society in the act of *being itself*, and the pilgrims — the fictional individuals whose characters, appearances and behaviour are interrogated in the poem — are engaged in a communal activity expressing the fact that they are a society. (It would be interesting to speculate what might be a comparable contemporary activity.)

It has been fairly common to suppose that the main thrust of the *Prologue* is satirical — judging characters as they 'are' against what they 'should be', with the context of pilgrimage acting as a built-in yardstick, a reminder of ultimate values. Chaucer's poem does indeed remind us of the gaps which may exist between the symbolic value attributed to an action, and the actual performance of the action. (To travel on a pilgrimage by no means guarantees perfect spirituality in the traveller; general agreement within a society that pilgrimage is a good idea is not conclusive evidence of that society's absolute purity and wholesomeness.) An ideal society, however, can exist only in hopes, desires and aspirations — or in the symbols created to represent these. An actual society is formed partly out of aspirations and expectations but mainly out of the complex 'fit', at any moment in its history, between the various roles available within it and the ways in which actual individuals fill or perform those roles: it is the nature of this 'fit' which is explored in Chaucer's *Prologue*. By bringing to the foreground from the very start the mixed motives for pilgrimage itself, the poem declares its intention to deal less with what 'should be' in society than with what actually *is going on* — what kinds of thing prove in fact to be valued, tolerated or denied in a society such as that which these pilgrims comprise?

It is perhaps significant that the portrait of the Knight comes first in the *Prologue*. For the status and respect accorded to this dignified, rather 'heavyweight' figure — which appear at first sight to be the natural and deserved consequences of his conduct and character — are in fact revealed as having rather more to do with the motives and attitudes of others in his society: motives and attitudes as mixed as those which we have seen to underlie the activity of pilgrimage. For while our narrator's tone here is thoroughly approving, and while it seems clear enough that by his fellow-pilgrims the Knight is applauded as a 'verray, parfit gentil' (l.72) exponent of his profession, what seems not so clear as we read on into the poem is the relevance to the majority of the other pilgrims of this knightly calling and the values it symbolises. Few enough of them show any sign of wishing to emulate his exemplary service and humility.

The function of the Knight in his society seems thus to be identified as that, primarily, of a figurehead — a visible embodiment of values to which everyone can pay lip-service, but to which few of these pilgrims would actually wish to commit themselves, or to be reminded of too closely in their daily lives. Questions as to whether the Knight himself is as decent and sincere as he seems (or whether for instance, as some critics have suggested, he may have been involved in some mercenary operations) are virtually irrelevant; so long as someone is there to fill the role of crusading knight and to give a high profile to 'traditional values', the rest can pat themselves on the back for belonging to a Christian, chivalrous society, pride themselves on its standards of courtesy, fair play . . . and so on. (Going on the occasional pilgrimage could be said to fulfil a very similar function.)

In this way, after first being — like our narrator — impressed, we are prompted to question what really is signified by the catalogue of exotic names which charts the Knight's campaigning history. Following the call of duty in far-distant places, he seems to have spent most of his life well outside the society which pays him such fulsome compliments; we might begin to wonder whether this is not because, in a sense, there is no real job for him at home. A scapegoat bears the burden of a community's sins, and dies with them; while the Knight's fate is nowhere near as drastic as that, it would perhaps not be going too far to see him as wandering in a kind of exile, carrying the burden of his society's neglected ideals.

Through the portrait of the Knight we are made aware of the gaps which can open up between the continuing performance of a traditional social role and society's current valuation of that role. Reading further into the poem, it becomes clear that this is a society in the process of change: it is the 'newe world' (l.176) and 'the newe jet' (1.682) which are beginning to count, in the sense of determining the rules for success in this society. Characters such as the Knight and the Parson (who are frequently read as exemplifying ideals at which other characters should be aiming) turn out to be the exceptions rather than the rule; unrepresentative, however admirable, and rather old-fashioned. The Knight is one of those left to enact a tradition which has lost the ability (if indeed this ever really existed) to direct the conduct of the society it is supposed to inspire. He travels with a small retinue which neatly symbolises the structure of that tradition (feudal society) — the apprentice ('bacheler' — 1.80) Squire, and the faithful Yeoman retainer — and here too we may read the same sense of a tradition which society has left behind. A rising class of bourgeois professionals and specialists (merchants, lawyers, doctors), whom we are to meet shortly, has begun to marginalise the aristocratic all-rounder (will the Squire, charming and lively as he is, amount to anything more than an elegant society playboy?), and already it is those such as the Summoner and the Pardoner who have their fingers most firmly on the pulse of day-to-day life.

While the Knight may have become marginal to his society, however, his case should not be seen as unique in the *Prologue*. His is not the only role where symbolic significance has become detached from day-to-day realities. As suggested by the central metaphor of pilgrimage, the Church is very much at the centre of the society of the *Prologue*. But as we have seen from the outset how the essential (spiritual/religious) purpose of pilgrimage is becoming separated from the activity itself — which seems to be turning into more of an event on the social calendar (like Christmas nowadays, some might say) — so we shall not be surprised to find similar gaps opening up elsewhere in the 'religious' community. The Church is clearly a major source of employment, but while traditional ideals of duty and service may still help to define (or name) the roles people take up within it, such ideals bear less and less relation to the performance of those roles. So, following the knightly trio in the *General Prologue* comes a sizeable posse of ecclesiastical characters, all by profession servants of the Church, and the vast majority of whom obviously fall far short of any spiritual ideal (in some cases, of most secular ones too). While the Knight's 'worthy' performance in a high-profile but virtually obsolete role helps draw attention and salve the communal conscience, corruption and indolence run rife in one of society's key institutions.

Now it is no doubt, unfortunately, true that most people in the real world are not as honest, sincere or dedicated as Chaucer's Knight is reputed to be. But at the same time it would hardly be satisfactory or adequate to explain all the corruption and the failings, which the *Prologue* identifies in its ecclesiastical figures, entirely by reference to supposed elements within the individual psychology, or 'character', of each of them. To criticise those such as the Prioress/Monk/Friar in terms of shallowness, selfishness, greed or callousness perhaps brings into play a relevant vocabulary, but it does not give an *explanation* of what is going on, merely another kind of description.

We have to remind ourselves that these are fictional creations, not actual historical beings; the reasons for their being as they are — or as we read them — are to be sought first within the poem. The 'behaviour' of any 'character' in the text must therefore be described and judged primarily in terms of the patterns and structures formed by the text itself — not by apparently common-sense formulations such as 'that's what monks in Chaucer's time were actually like', or 'this woman had the wrong sort of personality for a nun', which take us immediately outside the borders of the text. We may of course wish to open these borders at a later stage in our dealings with the text, in order to consider it in some kind of wider context.

Within the controlling metaphor of pilgrimage, the *Prologue* constructs character in terms of social interaction. That is to say, the poem explores and demonstrates interrelations and interactions between people who see themselves as a group, and the frequently ambiguous, contradictory results of these transactions as they appear through individual members of the group. How, for instance, do the responsibilities of a Prioress come to be ignored in the way described in lines 118–162? Not, surely, through the force of character ('triviality'?) of that one woman alone. How can a community tolerate such flouting of rules and traditions as that indulged in by the Monk — and even, apparently, applaud it? (He is considered 'to been an abbot able' —

l.167.) In the same way, presumably, as that same society shows no inclination to denounce or disown a Friar who affirms that:

> . . . unto swich a worthy man as he
> Acorded nat, as by his facultee,
> To have with sike lazars aqueyntaunce.
> It is nat honest, it may nat avaunce,
> For to deelen with no swich poraille,
> But al with riche and selleres of vitaille.

(ll.243–248)

These abuses clearly cannot be blamed entirely on individual character defects. They are both an effect and, in turn, partly a cause of that process of continuous interaction between individuals, roles and expectations to which is given the label 'society'.

Analysis of such a process is clearly a complex business, and in commenting on the pilgrims and their society it would certainly be easier to fall back on conventional categories of 'character', or to talk in terms of the hierarchies of feudal society, or the gradations of sinfulness so precisely classified by the medieval Church. Then it might seem straightforward enough to prove that (say) the Friar is more culpable than the Prioress. (She may be silly and trivial, but she does not actively cause harm in the same way as do the Friar's neglect of the sick and the poor, and his debasement of the sacrament of confession.) The structure of the *Prologue*, however, constantly requires us to explore interconnections and juxtapositions, to circle back and forth through the text and to realise how the behaviour, the strengths and weaknesses of any one character are intimately bound up with those of others. So — to pursue the example of the Prioress and the Friar, for instance — it is failures of leadership and responsibility at one level (such as hers) which allow and encourage those at other levels (such as his) to get away with what they do. Correspondingly, it is easy to suppose that, should the Prioress ever suffer from pangs of conscience, she will surely comfort herself with the knowledge that at least she is not actually corrupt in the way that so many others are.

So far, we have concentrated on just a few specific examples from the early sections of the poem; there is not space here to analyse in such terms the whole poem. But the structure of the *Prologue* is perhaps becoming clear: each portrait 'plays off' all the others, in a complex network of comparison and contrast. The behaviour of each individual helps to explain, and is in turn partly explained by, that of others. Each portrait reveals not just an individual, but another twist in the fibres which weave together into the texture of a society. To help to alert us to this structure in the *Prologue* there are many textual features, existing at all levels, from individual words (try 'worthy', for instance, with all its repetitions and subtle variations), to larger recurrent themes such as material greed, the use and abuse of talents, or success and reputation.

In our discussion we have seen the society of the *Prologue* mainly in terms of the marginalising of 'traditional' values, as evidenced in an activity (pilgrimage), an individual (the Knight) and an institution (the Church). A full consideration of the poem would have to take account also of the new order which is replacing those traditions — the order of bourgeois professionals and specialists, as I called some of them earlier on. It would be illuminating, too, to examine in detail other individuals and their roles — such as the Clerk, for instance, poised at the moment of choice between 'benefice' and 'office' (ll.291, 292); what are the incentives and pressures (the 'values'?) in his society which might sway him either way? And what about (say) the Wife of Bath, whose abundant energies seem to have been left almost entirely untapped by her society? (The reference to her 'wandrynge by the weye' — l.467 — may contain a moral euphemism, but also accurately pinpoints a character whose role in society is marginal. Interestingly, like the Knight, she has spent much of her time abroad.)

Finally there is (as there was at first) our narrator, the ever-present 'I' who is of course central to the structure of the poem, conducting us around the 'compaignye/ Of sondry folk' (ll.24–25). At times a shadowy, chameleon-like figure, subordinating himself to the personalities of those he meets ('And I seyde his opinion was good' — l.183), at other points he steps forward to articulate explicit judgements, with which apparently we are expected to agree. But, as always, we remember that we are dealing with a text, and that this narrative 'I' is constructed as a character within it. We hear, not the unmediated voice of

Chaucer the poet, but the voice of a fictional character who in the opening lines of the poem has placed himself firmly within the fictional society that he describes: 'I was of hir felaweshipe anon.' (1.32). His responses — the expectations, approval and regrets he expresses or implies in the course of his account of the society of the pilgrimage — are as much a part of the texture of that society (and of the *text* of that society) as are the subjects of the portraits he presents to us. Nonetheless, we might be a little surprised to find that, after all the corruption, selfishness, indolence and laissez-faire that he has observed and noted, he can still end his description by celebrating unity and togetherness, in the 'oon assent' (ll.777, 817) which is apparently arrived at by the pilgrims. But then we realise that all they have agreed on is — to tell each other a lot of stories. And isn't that just what they are doing all the time, really?

AFTERTHOUGHTS

1

What does Norgate see as the symbolic significance of pilgrimage?

2

Compare Norgate's commentary on the Knight (pages 11–14) with that of Oliver (pages 83–86) and Moseley (page 114).

3

'We have to remind ourselves that these are fictional creations, not actual historical beings' (page 14). Why?

4

What do you understand by Norgate's contention that 'the *Prologue* constructs character in terms of social interaction' (page 14)?

Alan Gardiner

*Alan Gardiner is a Lecturer in English
Language and Literature at Redbridge
Technical College, and is the author of
numerous critical studies.*

ESSAY

The poet as pilgrim: the narrator of the *General Prologue*

With many of the Canterbury tales there is a dramatic relationship between tale and teller: the story the pilgrim tells repays
study not only as a story in its own right but also as a revealing
expression of the pilgrim's character. *The Pardoner's Tale*, for
example, has been acclaimed as one of the greatest short stories
ever written, but read in conjunction with *The Pardoner's
Prologue* it is also a penetrating examination of the complex
personality of the Pardoner himself. Does a similar relationship
exist between the *General Prologue* and its pilgrim-narrator?
Some critics have certainly thought so, and have argued that the
narrating voice of the poem belongs to a consistent, credible
character — 'Chaucer the pilgrim' (an expression first used by
E T Donaldson in 1954), someone we should be careful not to
confuse with Chaucer the poet. The object of this essay is to
consider the validity of such an approach and the nature and
purpose of Chaucer's narrative technique.

Chaucer appears to offer little encouragement to those
seeking to furnish his pilgrim-narrator with a distinct, rounded

character. Whereas the narrator gives us detailed descriptions of his fellow-pilgrims — of their 'condicioun', 'degree' and 'array' — he says nothing of his own background or appearance. However, this in itself is perhaps intended to imply something about his character — that he is diffident and self-effacing. Such an interpretation would certainly be consistent with his apologetic confession late in the poem:

> Also I prey yow to foryeve it me,
> Al have I nat set folk in hir degree
> Heere in this tale, as that they sholde stonde.
> My wit is short, ye may wel understonde.

> (I, ll.743–746)

It is also consistent with the presentation of the pilgrim-narrator elsewhere in *The Canterbury Tales*. When he is called upon to tell his tale the Host remarks on his shyness ('For evere upon the ground I se thee stare') and his 'elvyssh' countenance (VII, ll.697, 703). He is however sufficiently outgoing to strike up an acquaintanceship with his fellow-pilgrims, speaking to each of them and accepted by them as a member of their party (I, ll.30–32). But his attitude in the *General Prologue* portraits towards most of the pilgrims he describes suggests his sense of his own inferiority. He shares the high opinion so many of them have of themselves and is full of admiration for their attributes and abilities. Often his praise of them appears undeserved (as when a character such as the Merchant is described as 'worthy') or implies approval of what ought to be condemned (the Friar's ability to extract money from the poorest widow, for example). There is an apparent blindness to the shortcomings of the characters, indicating that the narrator is to be seen as naïve and incapable of sound moral judgements. With some pilgrims he is less respectful: the Man of Law 'semed bisier than he was' (I, l.322), the effeminate Pardoner is contemptuously compared to 'a geldyng or a mare' (I, ll.691). E T Donaldson (in his essay 'Chaucer the Pilgrim') sees a consistency and a pattern here also. He argues that the pilgrim-narrator is a member of the bourgeoisie, elaborately deferential towards the upper-class pilgrims but more confident and outspoken in his descriptions of those of lower rank. The admiration he does express for the middle- and lower-class pilgrims is centred mainly upon their wealth, their possessions and their skill at making money, reflecting the narrator's own materialist values.

The argument that the *General Prologue* is narrated throughout by a believable and clearly discernible 'character' has its weaknesses however. The fiction that the narrator is travelling with the pilgrimage and simply reporting what he sees and hears on the journey is not maintained consistently. Information is included in his portraits that could not possibly have been obtained in this way. If the Merchant covered up his financial difficulties so successfully that 'Ther wiste no wight that he was in dette' (I, l.280), how did the narrator come by this knowledge? How did he know that the Knight:

> . . . nevere yet no vileynye ne sayde
> In al his lyf unto no maner wight?

(I, l.70–71)

The notion of a gullible, slow-witted narrator who is blind to the moral failings of his companions also has its inconsistencies. It is strange that a narrator who cannot perceive the glaring moral deficiencies of certain pilgrims should be so alive to the moral strengths of others. The portrait of the Parson, for example, is full of explicit recognition of the character's virtue, often in terms that imply a condemnation of those members of the Church who fall short of his standards: 'riche he was of hooly thoght and werk./ . . . He was a shepherde and noght a mercenarie./ . . . He waited after no pompe and reverence' (I, l.479, 514, 525). Are we to believe that this is the same narrator who said of the corrupt Friar, 'Ther nas no man nowher so vertuous' (I, l.251), and applauded the Monk as 'A manly man, to been an abbot able' (I, l.167)?

In the Parson's portrait the narrating voice appears to be not that of Chaucer the pilgrim but that of Chaucer himself. The same can be said of the portraits of the Knight and the Plowman. Chaucer may adopt the guise of a naïve, impressionable pilgrim, but he occasionally allows the mask to slip. The pilgrim-narrator is employed in the *General Prologue* as a literary device, but the way in which the device is used is not rigidly schematic and we should not expect every line in the poem to correspond to the idea we have of the narrator's 'character'.

Given that Chaucer did, for much of the poem at least, conceal himself behind the figure of a pilgrim-narrator, there remains the question of why he chose to adopt such a technique — what are its advantages as a narrative device? To an extent he was simply adhering to a convention much followed by himself and other medieval poets. In many medieval poems there is a narrator whose character has little in common with the poet who created him. The device is particularly associated with medieval dream poetry, in which the subject of the poem is a dream or vision experienced by the narrator. The most important and influential poem in this tradition is the French *Roman de la rose*, which was written in the thirteenth century and which Chaucer is believed to have translated. As in other dream poems, the dreamer finds himself transported to a beautiful, exotic world, through which he wanders with the aid of a supernatural guide. Chaucer's first poem in the tradition, and his first major original work, is *The Book of the Duchess*. In this and all his subsequent major poetry Chaucer recounts the story through the medium of a simple, gullible narrator. In *The Book of the Duchess* the narrator falls asleep over a book, dreams he sees a hunt taking place and then that he is led by a small hound into a forest, where he meets a knight dressed in black. The dreamer is bewildered by his new surroundings and confused by the conversation he has with the knight. Other dream-poems by Chaucer are *The House of Fame* and *The Parliament of Fowls*. In the former, the narrator is guided through the strange world of his dream by an eagle which flies along with the dreamer in its claws. In *The Parliament of Fowls* the narrator dreams he is in a beautiful garden, where he witnesses the supposed annual meeting at which birds choose their mates. In both *The Book of the Duchess* and *The House of Fame* the innocent, perplexed narrator is a source of comedy, much as in *The Canterbury Tales* Chaucer invites his audience to laugh at his depiction of himself as a wide-eyed simpleton. *Troilus and Criseyde*, Chaucer's longest complete work, is not a dream-poem but Chaucer again uses a naïve narrator to relate the events of the story. The culmination of Chaucer's experimentation with this technique is of course *The Canterbury Tales*, in which each of the stories has a different narrator. With some of the tales we are in fact scarcely aware of the narrator's existence, and there does not appear to be a strong or complex relationship between the tale and its teller. With others, and with the *General Prologue*, the narrator has an important, discernible presence and plays a significant part in determining our response to the text.

In the *General Prologue* Chaucer's manipulation of the narrator has a variety of effects. One of the most important is the comic irony which is directed against the pilgrims who are described in the portraits, against the pilgrim-narrator and against Chaucer himself. The narrator praises his fellow-pilgrims indiscriminately, oblivious of the moral flaws his accounts of them unwittingly reveal. The avaricious, unprincipled Physician is acclaimed 'a verray, parfit praktisour' (I, l.422), the perverted, hypocritical Pardoner is 'a noble ecclesiaste' (I, l.708), the morally repulsive Summoner 'a gentil harlot and a kynde' (I, l.647). He interrupts his explanation of the Monk's contempt for the rules of his order to tell us, 'And I seyde his opinion was good' (I, l.183). If monks remain inside the cloister, he asks, 'How shal the world be served?' (I, l.187) — instantly demolishing his own argument because a man who wanted to serve the world and not God should not become a monk in the first place. There is a similar interjection in the Manciple's portrait:

> Now is nat that of God a ful fair grace
> That swich a lewed mannes wit shal pace
> The wisdom of an heep of lerned men?

> (I, ll.573–575)

The suggestion that the Manciple's ability to swindle his employers is a gift of God only heightens our sense of the character's immorality. Often the narrator's approbation is immediately undermined by what follows it, as in the memorable couplet from the Wife of Bath's portrait:

> She was a worthy womman al hir lyve:
> Housbondes at chirche dore she hadde fyve

> (I, ll.459–460)

In the Friar's portrait we see the same technique in reverse: a veiled reference to the character's sexual promiscuity is followed by a line that is grotesquely inappropriate:

He hadde maad ful many a mariage
Of yonge wommen at his owene cost.
Unto his ordre he was a noble post.

(I, ll.212–214)

In all of these instances the narrator is as much a victim of Chaucer's irony as the character described. He is shown to be credulous and comically obtuse, and the poem becomes through his presence a satire on human fallibility. Chaucer also mocks himself. His medieval audience are likely to have been aware of a comic discrepancy between Chaucer the pilgrim-narrator and Chaucer the man. The simple, unsophisticated narrator is in marked contrast to the accomplished poet and successful man of public affairs we know Chaucer to have been. The poet offers us mocking self-portraits elsewhere in his work, as when the Man of Law prefaces his tale by observing:

> But nathelees, certeyn,
> I kan right now no thrifty tale seyn
> That Chaucer, thogh he kan but lewedly
> On metres and on rymyng craftily,
> Hath seyd hem in swich Englissh as he kan
> Of olde tyme, as knoweth many a man;
> And if he have noght seyd hem, leve brother,
> In o book, he hath seyd hem in another.

(II, ll.45–52)

When asked to tell his own tale, the pilgrim-narrator offers the feeble *Tale of Sir Thopas*, which with its banal content and trite rhymes parodies the worst metrical romances of Chaucer's day. The Host soon interrupts him, declaring that he can take no more of the narrator's 'rym dogerel' (VII, l.925). The narrator says he will tell instead 'a litel thyng in prose' (VII, l.937), and there follows the extremely lengthy *Tale of Melibee*.

The device of the naïve narrator is also crucial to the descriptive method of the *General Prologue* portraits, which is designed to give the impression of an *absence* of method. The pilgrim-narrator implies at the beginning of the poem that he is to adopt a systematic approach to his task:

> Me thynketh it acordaunt to resoun
> To telle yow al the condicioun

> Of ech of hem, so as it semed me,
> And whiche they weren, and of what degree,
> And eek in what array that they were inne
>
> (I, ll.37–41)

In other words, his portraits will contain information on the pilgrims' appearance, social rank and general character and circumstances ('the condicioun/ Of ech of hem . . . / And whiche they weren'). But while such information is usually given, the order in which it is presented appears entirely random. The portraits begin in a wide variety of ways and often with unceremonious abruptness:

> A KNYGHT ther was, and that a worthy man
>
> (I, l.43)

> A MARCHANT was ther with a forked berd
>
> (I, l.270)

> A SHIPMAN was ther, wonynge fer by weste
>
> (I, l.388)

> A good WIF was ther of biside BATHE,
> But she was somdel deef, and that was scathe.
>
> (I, ll.445–446)

The portraits as a whole do not conform to any consistent pattern and within each individual portrait there is a corresponding absence of structured description. We are told that the Wife of Bath has a red complexion but do not learn until ten lines later that she is gap-toothed; the lines in between tell us of her five marriages and her pilgrimages to Jerusalem, Boulogne, Galicia and Cologne. In each portrait there is an accumulation of apparently unrelated detail, which may include dress, personal history, attitudes and opinions, complexion, manner of speech, leisure activities, eating habits, professional competence. A particularly striking instance of the juxtaposition of incongruous detail occurs in the Cook's portrait:

> But greet harm was it, as it thoughte me,
> That on his shyne a mormal hadde he.
> For blankmanger, that made he with the beste.
>
> (I, ll.385–387)

This casual, haphazard approach accords perfectly with the employment of an artless, simple-minded narrator. The descriptions have a convincing naturalness and spontaneity: the narrator faithfully reports what he has seen and learnt but he is incapable of imposing any real order on his knowledge. He is also incapable of drawing conclusions from his observations, an incapacity which Chaucer plainly did not intend his audience to share. The small pieces of information that make up each portrait, seemingly random and often presented as if they were trivial and incidental, are usually the key to the character's true self. The narrator remarks without comment that the Physician 'kepte that he wan in pestilence' (I, l.442), but it is a telling disclosure that confirms the Physician's acquisitiveness and lack of compassion. Similarly, the company the Friar keeps (he was better acquainted with innkeepers and barmaids, the narrator innocently tells us, than with lepers and beggars) indicates his unsavoury life-style and disdain for those who ought to receive his charity.

As these examples illustrate, the reader must repeatedly supply the judgements which the narrator so conspicuously fails to make. The use of a naïve narrator is thus a means of securing the reader's active involvement in the poem. The information the narrator gives us about clothing, personal habits and so on is usually significant but it is left to us to decide what the significance is. We must also decide the effect that is achieved by the juxtaposition of particular details, and when the treatment of a character is ironic. It is similarly left to the reader to spot similarities and contrasts between the pilgrims. The narrator himself makes no explicit comparisons, though the portraits are full of revealing correspondences and dissimilarities. The Knight's sober maturity contrasts markedly with his son's youthful energy, but they share a willingness to serve. The Monk's string of fine horses emphasises the self-denial of the staff-carrying Parson, who travels around his parish on foot. The Clerk's disregard for material comforts is underlined by the contrast between his threadbare coat and the expensive clothing of other pilgrims.

But though judgements and conclusions are ultimately the responsibility of the reader, Chaucer subtly guides and influences our response. The order of the portraits, for example, invites comparisons of the kind made above: the impoverished Clerk is set amongst the prosperous middle-class pilgrims, the virtuousness of the Parson and his brother the Plowman is all the more apparent because their portraits are immediately followed by those of the thieves and scoundrels who make up the final group of pilgrims. As has been seen, the details of a portrait are often carefully arranged to heighten the irony. The narrator is evidently impressed by the Prioress's ability to speak French 'ful faire and fetisly' (I, l.124), but in the next couplet the impression of sophistication is undercut by the disclosure that she spoke it with a London accent. The narrator's belief that the Monk merited the position of abbot is contradicted in the very same line by the assertion that he was a 'manly man' (I, l.167).

On other occasions, however, the response that Chaucer intended is much less obvious. Chaucer's concealment behind the guise of the pilgrim-narrator makes a final evaluation of certain pilgrims difficult. Are we to approve of the Franklin's generosity and wholehearted enjoyment of life or deplore his gluttony? Is the Monk to be admired for his vitality or condemned for his neglect of his ecclesiastical duties — or both? The complex, contradictory attitudes we have towards these and other characters appear to have been shared by Chaucer. He was fascinated by the variety of human nature, and in the *General Prologue*, and *The Canterbury Tales* as a whole, he displays a sympathetic insight into a range of different approaches to life. Often he appears interested less in judging than in understanding. This does not mean that he shies away from moral judgements (his irony is often pointed, indeed savage) but that he is intensely curious about human motives, attitudes and behaviour — and the naïve but all-seeing narrator helps him to convey this.

AFTERTHOUGHTS

1

What inconsistencies does Gardiner point out in the narrative style of the *General Prologue*?

2

Do you agree that the method of the *General Prologue* is designed to give the impression of an *absence* of method' (page 24)?

3

What do you understand by 'the reader's active involvement in the poem' (page 26)?

4

'Often he appears interested less in judging than in understanding' (page 27). Do you agree?

John E Cunningham

John E Cunningham currently divides his time between writing and travel. He is the author of numerous critical studies, including 'The Prologue' to 'The Canterbury Tales': A Critical Study *(Penguin, 1985).*

ESSAY

Character and caricature in Chaucer's *General Prologue*

The pilgrims of the *Prologue* are commonly considered to fall into two types, excluding those, like the priests accompanying the Prioress, who are merely mentioned, not described at all: stereotyped representations of various trades, virtues and vices; and fuller 'characters', some of them perhaps pictures of people Chaucer actually knew. This division has led to a minor industry, the attempt by scholars to identify the pictures in this gallery with their originals; and has also engendered a lot of argument about which category some of the pilgrims belong to. It is the purpose of this essay to suggest that we may be looking at Chaucer from a viewpoint that he did not share with us in so approaching his work: that our notion of character and character-drawing differs considerably from his.

First let us briefly consider the problems of the system of classification suggested above. Even when a character is little more than mentioned — the five Guildsmen are a case in point, none of them being separately described — there may be more in them than meets our eye. The only descriptive detail we are given is that their knives, belts and purses were not mounted with brass but with silver (ll.366–368). Showy, we may think: the medieval listener would know rather more — these men were so keen on ostentation that they were prepared to break the Sumptuary Laws, which forbade silver ornaments except to men much richer than these were likely ever to be. One of the three priests, merely mentioned, as we have said, comes to life when he tells his tale, and we should do well to remember that the *Prologue* is — a prologue.

Its leading member, first described, first to tell his story, the Knight, is generally thought of as a stereotype: he represents the qualities of chivalry which were dying out when Chaucer was writing, with his old-fashioned mail coat that has stained his tunic with rust, his simple virtues, his piety, his sound but not showy horses and single attendant, just as his son, the Squire, represents the new age with his courtly attainments of literacy, composition, dancing and music (ll.95–96) added to his courage in the field. Yet some commentators have found the picture vivid and affectionate enough to suppose that it is a tribute to a real man, and have advanced names to fit. Others think the whole thing is too good to be true — that this is caricature, in fact — and have suggested a devious satirical purpose here: the Knight is, as some of his class, trained only for warfare, had become, a mere freebooter, out for blood and plunder, and the impressive list of his expeditions is ransacked for evidence of exploitation. We may feel that this approach is as extreme as that which says that the Merchant must be based upon a real London character, recognisable to Chaucer's courtly audience, because he goes out of his way (l.284) to say that he does not know the man's name. It may be true: it may equally be true that the poet was filling out a couplet with a handy rhyme, something he was not above doing now and then.

If the Merchant is a stereotype, it is, of course, that of the unscrupulous businessman whose life is governed by the need to make money. This is a less attractive quality in the Doctor — who saved the money he made when there was an outbreak of plague and is ironically said to be especially fond of gold because it is a stimulant to the heart in medicine (ll.442–444) — yet it is in his description that we find the key to the medieval notion of character which we wish to examine and compare with our own.

Most of us probably believe that our individual nature is the result of a combination of elements: our genetic inheritance and the influence of the environment in which we were brought up. We also know that our behaviour can be influenced by our bodily health and will probably have experienced the adolescent upheavals which go with temporary glandular imbalance. Chaucer believed something not very different, but based upon rather different assumptions. Our nature is complex, and his word for a man's character was his 'complexion', which in the course of time has come to mean merely the outward colouring, still taken to be some indication of the inner man. What we inherited, however, was not a DNA code but the juxtaposition of the planets at the moment of our birth in relation to the spot where that event took place; and instead of hormones, he believed in what he called humours. The Doctor, we are told, was an expert — because he understood astrology (l.414) and because he knew the origin of every illness and in which of the four bodily fluids or humours it was seated (ll.419–421). It was the mixture of yellow and black bile, blood and phlegm, that made up someone's 'complexion', in which the predominance of one humour determined the final character as choleric, melancholy, sanguine or phlegmatic, words we still use today to indicate hasty emotions (nowadays, especially anger), introverted gloom, out-going optimism and action, and finally a cold, stolid nature. Of these four types, Chaucer names only two in specific terms — we are told that the Franklin was sanguine, the Reeve choleric — but it was not necessary to put a name to what his audience would easily recognise. What is important for us to realise about this system, which was a couple of thousand years old when he used it, is that it looks at people as types.

The Doctor's interest in humours was because their disturbance was supposed to be the origin of disease, and he used astrology to determine the correct time to administer his remedies. We are told (l.438) that he studied the Bible very little, for he was concerned only with bodies, not with that one, unique possession, the soul — the soul which, born upon earth only once, was often to return to the eternal judgement of God before it had dwelt as much as one year in its body: medieval infant mortality was very high. Chaucer does not concern himself with souls any more than the Doctor does, though he had sharp words for those whose care this should properly be, and planned that *The Canterbury Tales* should end with a sermon by the poor Parson on how to avoid the sins that damned us: his concern with the humours and with astrology, in which he was proficient enough to be able to write a text book on the use of the astrolabe for his little son, was because they gave him a way of classifying and understanding men and women. His most vivid pictures are, as we shall see, in a sense 'types', but it is perhaps part of his greatness that he could sometimes do rather more.

How did he set about these portraits? First of all, it is surprisingly seldom that we are really told what a character looked like. When we are it is highly effective. Thus the Miller, thick-set, with beard to match, red hairs sprouting from the wart on his nose, flaring nostrils and (in every sense) big mouth, comes off the page at us in his coarse and fleshy self. The last two pilgrims to be mentioned, the Pardoner and Summoner, are also elaborately and unpleasingly described. But Chaucer is more likely to pick on just one or two details that he sees as significant, and part of our difficulty in reading him is that we may not always catch the meaning of what he has chosen. Thus the Prioress is fairly fully described, with her grey eyes and short, straight nose, but her creator says (l.154) that above all else she had a handsome forehead. Few modern writers would mention a woman's forehead in a description of her and many modern readers will have to think a little before they realise that this part of the Prioress should have been hidden by her coif. Good foreheads were fashionable at that time: she has one, and is vain enough — as she should not be in her calling — to show it off as shamelessly as the Wife of Bath shows off those close-fitting red stockings of hers that a more modest woman would have contrived to keep hidden.

The Wife is well worth exploring more fully, as we know much more about her personally than any other pilgrim, thanks to the enormous autobiographical prologue she later delivers to her own story, which is as long as the *General Prologue* itself. She is so vivid to us that we are likely to say that here, if anywhere, we have a real 'character', either based on someone Chaucer had met or brilliantly imagined. Yet she is a type and her personal appearance, apart from her large hips, takes up only a single line of description.

If we examine briefly the characteristics given as they arise in order (ll.445–476) we can see a lot of Chaucer's technique. First we are told that she was deaf, and that this was a pity. An odd beginning, perhaps suggesting that she talked more than she listened, this turns out much later to be part of a skilful design: the reason for her deafness was a blow from her husband — her fifth — about which, in due course, she tells us. Next comes her skill in weaving, and this is more important than it might seem: the Wife is the only unaccompanied woman in the group — even the Prioress, protected by the Church, has her retinue — and here is the explanation, or part of it. She was one of the few women of the time who could earn a living. We next learn that she was apparently a regular church-goer, but that what mattered to her there was her own social standing: she was angry if anyone went up to the altar in front of her and she dressed in elaborate headgear for this public occasion, wishing to be seen. On her stockings we have already commented, while the good footwear that goes with them is a sign of her prosperity. At last we reach the one line that describes her actual appearance as distinct from her clothes (l.458) in which we are told that her face was bold, handsome and ruddy. This is really quite vague. Yet to Chaucer's hearers it might well have suggested her temperament — probably sanguine, from her colouring — and in fact it foreshadows what she herself is much later to explain: her astrological influences. She tells us in her own prologue that she was born under a combination of Mars and Venus, so she is good-looking because of the latter and bold and ruddy because of the former; a typical product, in fact, and this extends to what she has later to tell us in her story, for despite her highly assertive nature (from Mars) her conclusion, as a daughter of Venus, is that a happy marriage is the best thing possible.

The description goes on to mention, tantalisingly, that she has had five husbands in the church porch, where weddings were then held, and has had other company in youth but there's no need to go into that now . . . an experienced lady, certainly, and we wonder what she will have to tell us about it all. Her extensive pilgrimages — no one except the Knight has travelled as much as she — suggest leisure and prosperity as much as devotion, and the widely spaced teeth, if that is what 'gat-tothed' means, were a sign of a roving nature. The gently paced horse she is riding would not need the pair of sharp spurs that Chaucer goes out of his way to mention, the only spurs he does. All horsemen then wore sharp spurs as a matter of course — hers are specified because she is a woman and they suggest her bold, mannish nature, as befits one born under Mars. Finally we are told she could chatter in company and she knew the remedies for love — one of which was marriage in which she is certainly expert — and all the tricks of that old trade. We have thus, in a few lines, been given a picture that is boldly coloured and interests us in what she might have to say. That we feel we should 'know' her if we met her is *not* a sign that Chaucer has created an individual but that he has well portrayed a type: we recognise the Wife because we probably have met her lookalike — middle-aged, a trifle overweight, good-looking in a brassy way, experienced, a great chatterer, the life and soul of every package tour, she is with us yet.

Those who feel that there must be more to her than this have probably read her own story as well as this description. For eight hundred lines in her prologue she rattles on in a style that truly comes to life — and that reveals the missing element in the *General Prologue*. Most of us in trying to give life to a character would make him or her speak, and nobody speaks in the *Prologue* except the Host, who has no later story to tell: Chaucer keeps this most revealing quality for the tales, though here and there we are given a hint of what a pilgrim might speak about and how. Of the Merchant we are told (1.275) that his speech always tended towards the subject of his profits, while the Clerk, who is next described, always directs his speech towards moral rightness, and speaks briefly but with much compressed meaning and lofty sentiment (ll.306–307). By contrast the Miller (ll.560–561) was an obscene chatterer who told mostly dirty stories.

The only rider to Canterbury who is allowed to speak, the Host, has but a single line devoted to his appearance, which tells us that he was big and bright-eyed: yet his speech is so vigorously carried off that he comes completely to life. Hearty, repetitive, shrewd, he broaches the subject of the tale-telling contest with a mixture of vitality and flattery:

> Now, lordynges, trewely,
> Ye been to me right welcome hertely;

For by my trouthe, if that I shal nat lye,
I saugh nat this yeer so myrie a compaignye
Atones in this herberwe as is now.
Fayn wolde I doon yow myrthe, wiste I how.
And of a myrthe I am right now bythoght
To doon yow ese, and it shal coste noght.

(ll.761–768)

Across six hundred years the speech rings true.

Like the — we have to say — typical publican that he is,
the Host adjusts his speech according to whom he addresses:
thus he begins the instructions to draw lots by calling on the
man of highest rank present, the Knight, then the lady who
most fancied herself socially, the Prioress, speaking to each with
deference; the poor Clerk gets a rougher speech:

'Sire Knyght,' quod he, 'my mayster and my lord,
Now draweth cut, for that is myn accord.
Cometh neer,' quod he, 'my lady Prioresse;
And ye, sire Clerk, lat be youre shamefastnesse,
Ne studieth noght . . .'

(ll.837–841)

This charming little observance of the social nuances may
serve to remind us of one last, but highly important, difference
in our way of looking at character. 'Class' has become simul-
taneously a dirty word and one that people love to bandy about:
it has also become very nearly meaningless. In feudal times
people all knew who they were because they stood in a strictly
defined order of precedence — one that had to be well known to
a man who was, like the Host, worthy to marshal the guests in
their correct order in a dining-hall (l.752). Of course there are
always folk with pretensions to a higher place in the system and
Chaucer enjoys making fun of them, whether it is the Prioress
whom we have just mentioned, with her affected, courtly French
speech and manners, or the Guildsmen with whom we began our
investigation, with their silver trappings and wives who liked
being addressed as 'Madam'. But in general Chaucer did not
need to introduce definitions of class into his characters'
portrayal as these were already understood by his audience.
Some of the signs are there, however, if we can read them.

The Reeve, for example, such a terror to tenant farmers, has his hair cut short round his ears and the top and front are shaven like a priest's tonsure (ll.588–590). One other character is mentioned as having short hair — the Yeoman — and from him we might guess the truth, that it was a sign of servile status: though he is quite prosperous, with his fine house on a heath, the Reeve is a lord's servant only. We ourselves often judge character — and period too, especially when watching old films — from hair styles, and Chaucer does this most effectively with the Pardoner:

> This Pardoner hadde heer as yelow as wex,
> But smothe it heeng as dooth a strike of flex;
> By ounces henge his lokkes that he hadde,
> And therwith he his shuldres overspradde;
> But thynne it lay, by colpons oon and oon;
> But hood, for jolitee, wered he noon,
> For it was trussed up in his walet.
> Hym thoughte, he rood al of the newe jet
>
> (ll.675–682)

This combines a practice still often seen in balding men of making a little go a long way, with an unpleasant vanity and inappropriate showing off — he is a preacher, after all, and should be both modest and shorn.

We may end by comparing with Chaucer's a typically modern way of judging a man's status (we rarely apply it to women) and indeed his character as well — and that is his means of transport, in which it appears that we are just as much classifiers as Chaucer was. The possession of certain makes of car is deemed to tell us a lot about the owners — indeed, new models are carefully researched with this in mind. Chaucer does not have brand-names on which to draw, but all the pilgrims were mounted — some perhaps hiring from the 'wide stables' of the Tabard — and the Shipman's nag (about the best we can do with the old word 'rouncy'), the Clerk's half-starved beast as skinny as a rake, the Wife of Bath's comfortable ambler, the hunt-loving Monk's elegant horses and jingling, decorated bridle, the Knight's mounts, good but not showy — all of these in a quiet way tell us something at least of the position of the riders: we even hear how one or two of them rode — the Shipman as best he could, sailors on horseback still being thought of as fish out of water, the self-important Merchant high in his saddle, the Wife of Bath easy in hers as befits someone who has travelled so widely, the handsome young Squire who not only rode well but sat a horse well too, a different matter.

It is no derogation of Chaucer's skill to say that he dealt largely in types: on the contrary, the more we explore the different ways in which he goes about introducing his varied cast, the more we may admire his mastery of subtle detail. This is why his characterisation, whether we think of it as individual or classifying, is so effective, rising far beyond the formal list of attributes which he had probably been taught when he studied rhetoric, beyond the four basic types of man and woman that the humours present, beyond simple, physical description, of which, as we have seen, there is surprisingly little. Perhaps our surprise — at realising, for instance, that the Host has only one line that actually describes him, the Wife of Bath one and a half — is the best tribute of all to Chaucer's craft.

AFTERTHOUGHTS

1

What do you understand to be the difference between a character and a caricature?

2

What distinction does Cunningham draw in this essay between medieval and twentieth-century notions of character?

3

'Chaucer does not concern himself with souls any more than the doctor does' (page 31). Do you agree?

4

Is it helpful to compare Chaucer's Wife of Bath with a modern stereotype, 'the life and soul of every package tour' (page 34)?

Pat Pinsent

Pat Pinsent is Principal Lecturer in
English at the Roehampton Institute of
Higher Education.

ESSAY

Chaucer's critique of the Church in the *General Prologue*

It is almost impossible for the modern reader, looking at the fourteenth century from a perspective which necessarily includes the Protestant Reformation of the sixteenth century and everything which has happened subsequently, to understand — much less to share — the view of the Church and Christianity held by Chaucer. His obvious awareness of abuses, which in the *Prologue* is displayed particularly in his depictions of the Monk, the Friar and the Pardoner, seems to match ill with the simple piety of his 'ABC'. This poem in honour of Mary, the mother of Jesus, may be the earliest of his surviving works. Its stanzas begin in turn with the letters of the alphabet in sequence; it commences, 'Almighty and al merciable queene'. A later work which reveals that this piety was not outgrown by the mature poet is the 'Retraction' at the end of the *Tales*, where he begs to be forgiven for his 'worldly vanitees' which include any of 'the tales of Caunterbury . . . that sownen into synne'. This piety appears to clash with the often bawdy material and ironic pose of many of the *tales*, so that the reader may be tempted to use the term 'hypocrite', one which scarcely does justice to the complexity of Chaucer's religious views.

The Catholic Church of the fourteenth century also defies simple description. There was a strong clerical stress on the Sacraments being indispensable for salvation, with an emphasis on individual confession, and this inevitably enhanced the power of the clergy. Yet the same period is one of strong popular devotion, as evidenced by the Mystery Plays, and is also the age of the great religious mystics such as Julian of Norwich. Movements for reform of the Church and the desire for the Bible to be more readily available in English were spearheaded by the translations of Wycliffe (1320–1384) and by the itinerant groups of preachers who came to be known as Lollards. They sought to bring the vernacular scriptures to churches and market-places, but at this stage probably had no wish to leave the Catholic Church.

That Chaucer was alert to the abuses is clear, especially in the *General Prologue* and *The Pardoner's Prologue and Tale*, yet to deduce from this that he was a Protestant before his time or, alternatively, that his devotion to religion and the Catholic Church was hypocritical, would be equally dangerous. It is my intention in this essay to look closely at his portrayals of those pilgrims whose professions were most obviously dependent on the Church, in order to present a case that what emerges is Chaucer's informed, committed, view of what the Church could, and should, become.

One caution, however, is essential. Because Chaucer portrays himself as one of the pilgrims, it is always tempting to take the 'I' who speaks so frequently throughout *The Canterbury Tales* as the voice of the poet himself. In fact, Chaucer delights in making use of a person who may share some attributes with the writer himself but is obviously far less acute. When the Host prevails upon him to tell a tale like the rest, he produces a number of stanzas of doggerel in *The Tale of Sir Thopas*, a romance which is so unpromising that he is not allowed to finish it, followed by the prose moralising of the lengthy *Tale of Melibee*. He is thus revealed as a tedious bore incapable of recognising his own deficiencies. In fact, the language used in the poetry itself often leads the reader to make judgements quite different from these voiced by the 'I' figure.[1]

It is useful, while considering the view presented of the Church, to observe that the *Tales* present a pilgrimage, 'The hooly blisful martir for to seke' (l.17). No doubt much of the value to Chaucer of choosing this format lies in the obvious advantage of the journey, enabling a semi-dramatic presentation of characters with their own voices to tell a fascinating range of stories. Nevertheless, their quest is a religious one, and, incidentally, is made to the shrine of an ambivalent figure, Thomas of Canterbury, who died because of resisting Henry II's intrusion on the rights of the Church. Thomas's martyrdom not only asserted the independence of the Church from the Crown, but also led to an immense amount of wealth coming into the hands of clergy in Canterbury. In the absence of any description of the pilgrims' arrival in the city, we can have no idea of whether or not Chaucer might at some stage have intended to use this fact. We can, however, at the very least say that here we have a religious journey to honour a religious death which had indirectly led to the amassing of wealth by the Church and thus to some degree of corruption in the very body which the martyr had died to preserve. In this light, can references to the 'blisful martir' be taken entirely at their face value, especially when spoken by the Host (l.770), who reveals himself as a strongly secular figure? The ambivalent religious quest, then, provides an ironic backdrop to Chaucer's depiction of a number of pilgrims whose professions are dependent on the Church. This dependence may be direct, as in the case of members of religious orders, such as the Prioress, or it may result from their employment by an ecclesiastical body, as in the case of the Summoner.

Throughout *The Canterbury Tales*, both in description of the pilgrims and in the tales they tell, the interaction between the religious and secular worlds is frequent, and it is clear that no rigid distinction can be drawn between the sacred and the profane. Within the *Prologue*, the significance of the Church is perhaps most apparent in the descriptions given of three groups

---

[1] A useful discussion of this distinction is to be found in E Talbot Donaldson, 'Chaucer the Pilgrim', *PMLA* LXIX 1954, pp. 928–936; reprinted in *Chaucer Criticism*, vol. I, ed. R Schoeck and J Taylor (Indiana, 1960).

of pilgrims. These are: three members of religious orders, the Prioress, the Monk and the Friar (ll.118–269); the Parson and the Plowman (ll.477–541); and the Summoner and the Pardoner (ll.623–714). These important passages, if examined closely, display notable variations in the ways in which these pilgrims are presented. It appears to be part of Chaucer's technique that the rather naïve 'I' who occasionally comments during these passages has a rather different stance in each section.

Chaucer's irony is perhaps most evident in the first of these passages, though it might, I suspect, be quite possible for an uninformed modern reader to take the portrayal of the Prioress, the Monk and the Friar as uncritical. The Prioress might seem to be one of the pilgrims with whom the more fastidious twentieth-century taste might be most at home. With her mild oaths (l.120) (but should she have been swearing at all?), her good singing of 'the service dyvyne' (l.122), her command of French 'ful faire and fetisly,/ After the scole of Stratford atte Bowe' (ll.124–125) (the reader may not realise that this probably disparages her accent), her delicate eating and her love of animals ('a mous' — l.144 — and 'smale houndes' — l.146), she seems attractive. Descriptions like 'She was so charitable and so pitous' (l.143) and 'And al was conscience and tendre herte' (l.150) can easily be read at their face value. It is only later, perhaps, that we begin to ask ourselves if we are expected to accept without question the apparent praise of a nun, who should be devoted to God, for accomplishments more appropriate to an elegant society lady. Would a medieval audience, accustomed to the teaching that animals had no souls and were therefore outside the scheme of salvation, have approved quite so much of her deep love of these creatures and her feeding her dogs with expensive meat, when her religious profession should have led her first to the service of God and humanity?

Again, the portrayal of the Monk as 'A manly man, to be an abbot able' (l.167), engaging with enthusiasm in sports, might not initially come over as highly critical when the Monk's view that he should not be confined to his cloister (as his Rule demanded) is endorsed by the Chaucer persona: 'And I seyde his opinion was good' (l.183). The description of his rich garments and devotion to comfortable living contains no explicit censure, although the association of his head with 'a forneys of a leed'

(1.202) may subtly warn of danger because it implies excessive heat.

The Friar is also presented with apparently favourable epithets, as in:

> Ful swetely herde he confessioun
> And plesaunt was his absolucioun

(ll.221–222)

His knowledge of the taverns is commended by the Chaucer persona, in praising 'swich a worthy man as he' (1.243). It is perhaps only at second reading that we stop to wonder why he may have needed to have 'maad ful many a mariage/ Of yonge wommen at his owene cost' (212–213) or ask how consistent with holy poverty is his 'semycope' of 'double worstede' (1.262).

Chaucer's technique in each of these portraits is, then, to appear to praise the ecclesiastical pilgrims for qualities which are either trivial and irrelevant to their holy profession, or totally opposed to it. He seems to use a kind of ascending order of irreligiousness, from the worldliness of the nun to the actual immorality of the Friar, but I would contend that readers are not left with a totally negative impression of even the worst of the three. Their vices are natural human weaknesses, which we have almost imperceptibly been led to approve of, or at least to tolerate. As we have gradually become conscious of their inadequacies, it is almost as if we too have been censured with them for our own deficiencies. This would probably have been still clearer to a medieval audience universally (at least in theory) obedient to the Church.

It is convenient to pass from these relatively mild censures on representative Church characters whose holy profession and worldly behaviour do not go together, to the section (ll.623–714) where Chaucer's criticism is more explicit, though it remains sufficiently humorous for the reader not to be totally alienated from the characters. The Summoner, whose function was to call delinquents before the ecclesiastical courts, is not, of course, himself a priest. His leading vice is probably hypocrisy, in calling offenders to justice while being corrupt himself. With his 'fyr-reed' face (1.624), his lechery, and the fact that 'Of his visage children were aferd' (1.628), he is certainly one of the least attractive of the pilgrims. The contrast here with the earlier passages where the negative features did not emerge so obviously means that the reader is from the beginning alienated from this man; Chaucer's technique is to make us judge the institution which employs him as well as the man himself. Corruption is within this institution; the courts, like the Summoner, are seen as being more concerned to extract money from sinners than to amend their conduct (ll.649–662):

> He wolde suffre for a quart of wyn
> A good felawe to have his concubyn
>
> (ll.649–650)

The Summoner is prepared, if properly bribed, to condone faults, but if the offenders are brought before the courts, he considers the financial aspect more important than the excommunication the courts can give: '"Purs is the ercedekenes helle," seyde he.' (l.658).

The Pardoner is probably, with the Wife of Bath, the best-known character among the pilgrims. It is difficult to be sure of the effect on the medieval audience of the occupation of any individual; it is probably more legitimate to assume the unpopularity of the Summoner than of the Pardoner, for the former's effect could be more devastating on the ordinary person. Our modern response to the Pardoner is influenced not only by the notoriety of Chaucer's creation even among those relatively unfamiliar with the *Tales*, but also by the scandal about the sale of indulgences, especially during Luther's time in the following century. Certainly there was some contemporary hostility towards Pardoners, but the way in which Chaucer seems to single this figure out, both in the *General Prologue* and in his own prologue and tale, is, I think, significant of the poet's desire for Church reform. The term 'gentil' (l.669) would almost certainly have been read as ironic in the fourteenth century, since the Pardoner's occupation is not that of a gentleman and he is clearly gentle neither in birth nor in character. Perhaps here again we have a discrepancy between the perception of the Chaucer persona and the judgement the poet seeks from his audience. Any doubts we may have as to how the poet is guiding our response are surely set at rest by the description, 'Swiche glarynge eyen hadde he as an hare' (l.684), particularly since the hare was a notoriously lecherous animal. Within his portrait, more than in those of any other of the pilgrims, even including his paramour the Summoner, there is direct criticism. When we read how 'with feyned flaterye and japes/ He made the person and the peple his apes' (ll.705–706), added force is given to the criticism by its relative proximity to the description of the Parson among the pilgrims (ll.477 ff). We naturally imagine the Pardoner deceiving a parson of similar virtue.

The irony of the description is heightened by the relative lack of emphasis on the falsity of the relics, in contrast with that which follows in *The Pardoner's Prologue and Tale*: the repeated 'he seyde' (ll.695, 696) is left to speak for itself, so that 'He was in chirche a noble ecclesiaste' (l.708) can come over as a not impossible statement from the 'I' persona. The poet, however, leads his reader to judgement: if this is the kind of behaviour approved by the institutional Church, as implied particularly by the term 'ecclesiaste', then the Church, not merely the Pardoner, is to blame.

Even without the further revelations given by the scurrilous nature of *The Summoner's Tale* and the self-disclosure of the Pardoner in his own prologue, Chaucer's presentation leaves us in no doubt of his condemnation, both of the two characters and, more significantly, of their occupations. Here we see a difference in degree of savagery from that in the passage discussed above (ll.118–270); the later passage, it can be claimed, conveys a direct censure of the fourteenth-century Church for its complacence about the evil of those who lived off it corruptly. The members of religious orders, the Prioress, Monk and Friar, have certainly been shown as less than ideal, but in their descriptions there seems no evidence that Chaucer is condemning the *original* spirit of their orders; the most that could be claimed is that there is a decline from the fervour of earlier ages and the rules are not being kept. About those who live off the Church, however, there is a different verdict: an institution which makes it possible for the venality of the Summoner and the deception of the Pardoner to thrive within an official ecclesiastical context needs some kind of reform of its structure.

I would however suggest that the kind of reform Chaucer

---

[2] See, for instance, the Prologue to Langland's *Piers Plowman*, ll.68–77.

wants is not totally radical, and for this claim my justification is based on an examination of the third section I mentioned above, the description of the Parson and the Plowman (ll.477–541). Unlike the portrayal of the members of religious orders, which damns by faint praise and irony, and that of the servants of the institutional Church, which condemns venality and corruption, this passage presents admirable characters. The reader who has become alert to irony is likely to read, 'A good man was ther of religioun' (l.477) and expect some comic deflation, at the least, to follow. However the use of biblical imagery about the sheep (l.508) and shepherd (l.514), and the criticism of the currently popular practice of seeking 'a chaunterie for soules' (l.510), in contrast with the Parson who 'sette nat his benefice to hyre' (l.507), all make it evident that our response to him should be favourable. The concluding lines:

A bettre preest I trowe that nowher noon ys.
. . . Cristes loore and his apostles twelve
He taughte, but first he folwed it hymselve

(ll.524–528)

reinforce the note of total sincerity. This is maintained in the description which immediately follows of his layman brother, the Plowman. To explore the significance of this occupation in fourteenth-century England would take too long[3] and reference can only be made here to Langland's *Piers Plowman*, where the complex symbolism associated with the character of Piers makes him both a representative human figure and, at times, a figure of Christ. While I am not suggesting that the Plowman would automatically be seen in ideal terms by a fourteenth-century audience (some negative portrayals do exist[4]), I would claim that by deliberately placing side by side at a central point in the *Prologue* these two virtuous men, closely linked in behaviour and kinship, Chaucer is putting particular emphasis on both of them. He is associating right action as displayed within a religious

---

[3] See for instance, relevant section in J Mann, *Chaucer and Medieval Estates Satire* (Cambridge, 1973), and J Coleman, *English Literature in History, 1350–1400* (London, 1981), especially pp. 23 ff and p. 279.

[4] For instance, Gower, in *Vox Clamantis*, quoted in R P Miller (ed.), *Chaucer: Sources and Background* (New York, 1977).

profession and that in secular life. Thus he is providing a contrast between the 'religious' characters whose descriptions are earlier than those of the Parson and the behaviour of the good priest. He follows this with a picture of the virtuous layman who behaves properly in regard to the Church: 'His tithes payde he ful faire and wel' (l.539), contrasting with the corrupt behaviour of the Church employees portrayed later in the *Prologue*. We have little doubt that the tithes the Plowman pays will be rightly used, for we have just read of the Parson who was:

> Ful looth . . . to cursen for his tithes,
> But rather wolde he yeven, out of doute,
> Unto his povre parisshens aboute
> Of his offryng and eek of his substaunce.
>
> (ll.486–489)

The Parson does not oppress his people even for what is his right, but gives to those in need in his parish; the Plowman, as well as help 'every povre wight' (l.537), has no hesitation in giving the Church its due. Having just witnessed the behaviour of the Parson, we have every expectation that what the Plowman gives will be used to relieve the poor.

The theme of pilgrimage which unites all these disparate characters provides reinforcement to the actual text, particularly when reference is made to the kind of tales which the characters tell. The Prioress, the Monk and the Friar seem to be on pilgrimage at least partly out of vanity. While *The Prioress's Tale* of little Hugh of Lincoln is unsavoury today, it does appear to be one of simplistic piety, revealing perhaps a woman of limited intellect despite her accomplishments. The Monk displays his learning in the area of secular narrative by telling tragic stories from biblical and classical sources. The Friar tells a tale directed against summoners and the Summoner retaliates by telling an equally dubious story against friars. Both of these tales could well be amongst those about which Chaucer felt the need to repent in his 'Retraction' (quoted at the beginning of this essay), but they serve the purpose of reinforcing the message conveyed by the description of these two characters. Both the Friar and the Summoner may be seen as seeking the applause of the group of pilgrims, such as the Host, the Miller and the Reeve, who see the journey primarily as entertainment.

The Pardoner's Tale about the three revellers who bring death upon themselves because of their inordinate love of money is, unlike most of those mentioned above, highly edifying, but its context within the kind of sermon he preaches makes its effect more complex. The tale is directed against avarice, regarded by most medieval moralists as the worst sin, and ironically the Pardoner's sermon in which he tries to extort money for his false relics is a flagrant example of this same vice, suggesting that his main motive for pilgrimage is the hope of gain from his fellow-pilgrims. Thus Chaucer's choice of such tales for characters who have already been seen as unsatisfactory seems fairly deliberate.

On the positive side, the Parson produces a long piece of edifying prose about the deadly vices and their correctives, which is generally placed at the end of the collection just before Chaucer's 'Retraction' of 'worldly vanitees'. The fact that the Plowman produces no tale cannot be used to support any argument in view of the fact that *The Canterbury Tales* is unfinished. We are, then, left with the impression that these two characters at least (as well as some of those not mentioned in this essay, such as the Knight) are on pilgrimage for the right kind of motive. They are on pilgrimage both in the literal sense and in the symbolic one of a religious quest through life. The teaching of *The Parson's Tale* against the sins is more efficacious because these sins have been so well displayed by some of his fellow-pilgrims both in their lives and in their own tales.

We may well conclude then that as well as being a useful framework for the presentation of description and narrative, the theme of pilgrimage to a shrine which by the late fourteenth century displayed both the original glory in the martyr's death and the later corruption of the Church may well have been deliberately chosen. Whatever Chaucer's motive for his 'Retraction', there is no reason to doubt that morality was part of his purpose in writing. He would have been very untypical of his age if he had not considered this important. Both the micro-structure of the *Prologue* and the macro-structure of the whole of *The Canterbury Tales* seem to display the aim of reforming the Church from within. From a negative point of view this is done by exposing the evils about which it was too complacent, in the religious orders and in the whole institution, but from the positive side Chaucer succeeds in revealing the potential for holiness it still offered, to both sacred and secular vocations.

AFTERTHOUGHTS

1

Why does Pinsent refer to the pilgrimage as an 'ambivalent' religious quest (page 41)?

2

Do you agree that readers are not left with a totally negative impression of the Friar (page 43)?

3

What distinctions are drawn in this essay between the presentation of the Summoner and the presentation of the Pardoner?

4

What do you understand by the terms 'micro-structure' and macro-structure' (page 48)?

Mark Spencer Ellis

*Mark Spencer Ellis is Head of English
at Forest School, and an experienced A-
level examiner. He has edited a number
of A-level texts.*

ESSAY

The Shipman's knife

Of all the vivid details we are given in the *General Prologue*,
the Shipman's knife is one of the most disturbing. Our glimpse
of it is just that, a glimpse:

> He rood upon a rouncy, as he kouthe,
> In a gowne of faldyng to the knee.
> A daggere hangynge on a laas hadde he
> Aboute his nekke, under his arm adoun.
> The hoote somer hadde maad his hewe al broun;
> And certeinly he was a good felawe.

> (ll.390–395)

The movement of the verse does not allow the attention to
linger; the knife is introduced in the second half of a couplet and
the momentum pushes the speaker on to the rhyming 'broun'
in spite of the full stop after 'adoun'. In the description of the
Shipman the opening eleven lines contain a tension between the
syntax and the rhyme which also mirrors the awkwardness of
his riding 'as he kouthe'. His dagger contrasts in every way with
those most recently mentioned, those of the Guildsmen:

> Hir knyves were chaped noght with bras
> But al with silver

> (ll.366–367)

These are ostentatiously paraded as marks of prosperity, not as functional instruments. But the Shipman's weapon is kept in exactly the right place for the brisk settling of scores. No time would be wasted fumbling with a belt, reaching down and pulling the dagger out. This blade is half hidden and at hand level for the quick draw and killing stab. The Shipman's knife points us to a decisive and brutal world. Embracing him as 'a good felawe' (1.395) has its element of risk if we contemplate the implications of being on the opposite side. And it is in the consequences of being on the opposite (losing) side that the description of the Shipman unites the syntax and the rhyme with the uncompromising couplet:

> If that he faught, and hadde the hyer hond,
> By water he sente hem hoom to every lond.

(ll.399–400)

This can be contrasted with other instances which may initially seem equally eye-catching. The Miller's wart, for example, is as vivid as could be hoped for. Right on the top of his nose with a clump of bristling red hairs sticking out, it forces itself into our imagination just as the Miller imposes himself on his fellow-pilgrims. Or one could take the fastidious table manners of the Prioress whose napkin was kept so busy that there wasn't the slightest trace of a mark seen in her cup when she had taken a drink. But there is a problem with offering these two as examples of the art of the *General Prologue*, and that is the brutal question which remains at the end of any analysis however thorough it may be; the question is simply 'so what?' Where does this detail lead us? The more we imagine the wart, the more vivid, the more wart-like it becomes, but the picture cannot take us to a world beyond it. The rhyme herys/erys (ll.555–556) followed by the heavy end-stop of a semi-colon makes the hairs on the wart a self-contained unit. It is not as if this physical characteristic grows out of a pattern of living in the way that the Monk's sleek and oily face or the ravaged mask of the Summoner all too clearly signal their particular life-styles. There is a sterility in the Miller's naturalistic wart; the detail serves to narrow the focus of our reading. The same applies to the Prioress's lip cleaning. The lady is not in competition with anyone else for the least stained lip award;

perhaps we can see in her actions the epitome of triteness, of behaviour which illustrates a determination to keep the concerns of her life removed from any pressing realities, but the final picture, the spotless rim of her cup, is almost photographic, naturalistic and static.

It is the realistic capacity to point us to a credible world beyond itself which makes a detail like the Shipman's knife so important. However, it is equally important to realise that this world is not 'background' against which timeless characters are paraded. The world to which the *General Prologue* points is the specific one of late fourteenth century England, the society from which the text cannot be separated.

One of the most straightforward adjustments we must make to our own received opinion of the world is to do with that most English of obsessions, the weather. We can regard a winter or March landscape as picturesque; so can anyone accustomed to warm clothing, warm houses and a potential diet varied enough not to seem seasonal. But an age when glazed windows were an expensive luxury does not see a bleak landscape as a 'view'. It speaks of monotonous diet, of cold, lack of comfort and little in the way of profitable work. The 'shoures soote' (l.1), of April mean fresh grass, fresh meat, new crops. It is dangerously patronising to categorise the opening of the *General Prologue* as 'conventional' or 'pastoral'. Certainly it draws on traditions found in other writing but we should see it as it directly relates to the way people lived at the time rather than as a quaint backcloth.

Details of individual pilgrims' characteristics and preferences are not a simple list for self-contained character sketches. The Monk, for example, loves hunting. He is 'a prikasour' (l.189), and his commitment to his sport is stressed by its financial aspect:

> Of prikyng and of huntyng for the hare
> Was al his lust, for no cost wolde he spare.

(ll.191–192)

It would be wrong to see the cost solely in terms of hounds, horses and equipment. The immediate clue to this is in the portrait of the professional forester, the Yeoman, whose job would include the vigorous protection of the game on his lord's estate. The Monk's outlay would cover the employment of similar tough men, totally proficient:

> (Wel koude he dresse his takel yemanly;
> His arwes drouped noght with fetheres lowe)
>
> (ll.106–107)

and additionally armed with 'a swerd and a bokeler' (l.112), and a murderously sharp 'gay daggere' (l.113). The Monk can afford to make as much noise as he likes with his jingling bridle; the preservation of his hunting is in the hands of those who melt into the background, perhaps 'in cote and hood of grene' (l.103). Hunting and the preservation of game in the late fourteenth century is a political act to be seen in relation to a volatile society which did indeed boil over in the Rising of 1381. Rosamond Faith explains:

> Although poaching obviously has an economic aspect, it seems to have had in the middle ages, as later, a vital though largely unspoken ideological aspect as well. The idea that the peasantry were entitled to what the land naturally provided conflicted with the seigneurial notion that lordship implied *dominium* over all the assets of the manor. . . . Poaching, primarily of deer, was a political issue in the late fourteenth century, and was seen as such by contemporaries. The Patent Rolls of the 1360s to 1380s are crowded with reports . . . of large-scale poaching raids on the property of the gentry, the aristocracy and the royal family, in which taking deer was combined with attacking manor houses, claiming common rights and burning manorial rolls.[1]

The ostentatious self-confidence of the Monk who parades the trappings of wealth, the sleeves 'purfiled at the hond/ With grys' (ll.193–194), and his boast that:

> Ful many a deyntee hors hadde he in stable
>
> (l.168)

constitute a challenge to anyone unwilling to accept the prevailing social structure. Society is not background; it is a shaping force.

---

[1] Rosamond Faith, 'The "Great Rumour" of 1377 and Peasant Ideology', in R H Hilton and T H Aston (eds), *The English Rising of 1381* (Cambridge, 1984), p. 67.

To describe this line as a boast needs justification. There are virtually no moments in the *General Prologue* when we can be certain that overt criticism of a character is clearly implied in the text; even the behaviour of the most appalling specimens is presented without absolute ethical judgement. In part this is because of our uncertainty about the 'Chaucer' figure who appears as narrator and pilgrim but an equally important point is the extent to which 'Chaucer' is almost a transparent reporter, carefully recording the pilgrims' introductions of themselves. The fiction of the *General Prologue* is a complicated one. We are asked to imagine that these 850 or so lines are part of a much greater whole and that they are written after each pilgrim had told not one but four tales. However, we are also aware that to begin with we are being rationed to a character sketch which does not embrace anything which may be revealed in the process of telling a tale or in the subsequent pilgrimage. And the first thing we have to 'believe' after accepting 'Chaucer' as our guide, is that what he is relating is in essence a series of self-portraits:

> And shortly, whan the sonne was to reste,
> So hadde I spoken with hem everichon
> That I was of hir felaweshipe anon

(ll.30–32)

Although there are pilgrims who could be the source of information about others — for example any one of the first three about each other, the Nun about the Prioress, or the Pardoner and the Summoner about each other — the fiction we accept is that of self-portraits filtered through the persona of 'I'. This effectively removes the possibility both of overt disapproval and of overt approval.

The element of the self-portrait does help us to come to terms with the very high proportion of pilgrims who seem to be at the top of their particular professional ladder. Sometimes the qualities attributed to them appear as unconditional compliments: 'ful plesaunt' (l.138), 'Sownynge in moral vertu' (l.307), 'ful riche of excellence' (l.311), 'In al this world ne was ther noon hym lik' (l.412). Two factors particularly contribute to our reading of this. One is that 'Chaucer' or 'I' is simply an uncritical reporter. The other is that it is perfectly credible for such a reporter to build up the status of acquaintances; to do so is to acquire a bit of reflected glory through knowing such people.

Nevertheless, there is a high proportion of the descriptions which contain an element of aggression and assertion. First there are the 'victimless' competitions whose function seems to be the enhancement of a particular pilgrim's status. No one else on the trip to Canterbury would feel slighted that the Knight's campaigning had covered more miles than anybody else's, 'no man ferre' (l.48); nor is there a pilgrim of comparable status to be goaded by the claims of where he had 'reysed':

> No Cristen man so ofte of his degree.'
>
> (l.55)

The same applies to the Franklin's generosity as a host:

> A bettre envyned man was nowher noon.
>
> (l.342)

The Miller's habitual winning of the ram 'At wrastlynge' (l.548) also poses no threat to any other pilgrim's self-esteem, nor would anyone wish to dispute the Wife of Bath's claim to precedence in 'the offrynge'(l.450) in her parish.

However, there is a clear pattern of more sinister aggression: aggression which fuels some of the most bitter exchanges in the link passages between tales. The apparently empty claim:

> Ther nas no man nowher so vertuous
>
> (l.251)

immediately becomes specific in the second half of the couplet:

> He was the beste beggere in his hous

The Friar's competitiveness is financial; he is determined to wring for himself the greatest possible part of a finite available sum, even the last farthing of a widow. While the rivalry between the Miller and the Reeve which breaks out after one tale is essentially a matter of the latter 'taking it personally', the bitter hatred between the Summoner and the Friar which dominates their respective tales is far deeper and is based in the way the two of them are rival predators. There is a ruthless exclusiveness in the way the Friar's patch is his and his alone:

> Noon of his bretheren cam ther in his haunt
>
> (1.252b)

The more we enter the world of commercial competition, the more the characters are portrayed in aggressive terms, an aggression which requires a victim. The Friar is simply trying to corner a limited market; the Manciple and the Reeve are out for profit. There is a surprisingly tough note in the portrait of the Manciple, a note which only becomes explicable when his social position and function are examined.   *Conning.*

That the Manciple knows exactly when to time his bulk-purchasing, 'ay biforn and in good staat' (1.572) may seem a straightforward claim to competence, and yet the next fourteen lines, two-thirds of the entire portrait, are given over to jeering at the lawyers at the Inn of Court whose financial shrewdness is nothing like as advanced as his. As the only quality ascribed to the Manciple is this particular form of sharpness, then it must be in these terms that he triumphed over the laywers and 'sette hir aller cappe' (1.586).

With the Reeve we are shown a world of miserable grasping misanthropy:

> Ther was noon auditour koude on hym wynne
>
> (1.594)

is a challenge to the future as well as a triumphant record. The implications of 'koude' are subtle; there is no overt admission of fraud but the suggestion that the Reeve starts from the same base as everyone else, and is, in theory at least, vulnerable if only someone knew how to get the better of him. The forceful graspingness is stressed in the way in which all of his lord's capital assets (ll.597–598) were '*hoolly* in this Reves gover-nynge' (1.599) (author's italics). The Reeve's superiority comes from his operating in a dehumanised world where he can make the correct assumption that anyone who might pose a threat to him must have a guilty secret:

> Ther nas baillif, ne hierde, nor oother hyne,
> Thet he ne knew his sleighte and his covyne.
>
> (ll.603–604)

The whole of this portrait is couched in aggressive terms: the 'cote and hood' (1.612) he receives as the traditional gift from his lord is presented in the context of his not having earned it through devoted and disinterested service. It is a joke that he is thanked for profiting at his lord's expense. The enjoyment derived from his well-situated house (ll.606–607) depends on its isolation from the unpleasant dwellings of the majority. The Reeve's absorption in profit understandably leads to his (self-imposed) isolation at the very end of the group.

As has already been shown, hunting and poaching were activities of major ideological significance at the time Chaucer was writing. Contemporary accounts show that lawyers, in particular justices, were a major target in the 1381 Rising. Recent work tends to stress the essentially conservative nature of the thought behind the Rising. Just as poaching was associated with an assertion of ancient rights seen by those who lived on and worked the land as threatened, so the whole class of lawyers were popularly associated with the removal of long-standing liberties. The point is not so much whether these rights and liberties had ever existed; what is important is the belief that any changes in society represented such an intrusion. Wat Tyler, one of the leaders of the Rising, is said to have demanded a commission 'to behead all lawyers, escheators and others who had been trained in the law or dealt in the law by reason of their office'.[2] Several of Chaucer's pilgrims would have been in considerable danger, and the popular force of the Manciple's boasting comes into sharp focus. The common view of lawyers was that of cheats whose training was directed at enforcing the removal of liberties and property rights:

> Ther koude no wight pynche at his writyng;
> And every statut koude he pleyn by rote.

(ll.326–327)

The Man of Law's knowledge is power, and it is paraded as competitive power. Like the Reeve, he throws down a challenge. He is acquisitive, and defies anyone to get the better of him in the extension of private ownership:

---

[2] Thomas Walsingham, *Historia Anglicana* (fourteenth century).

> Al was fee symple to hym in effect;
> His purchasyng myghte nat been infect.

(ll.319–320)

It is not surprising that his rural equivalent, the Franklin, who also had experience of presiding in court:

> At sessiouns ther was he lord and sire

(l.355)

chooses the Man of Law as his riding companion. The sense of aggressive challenge and assertion associated with the law is not a matter of personal idiosyncracy; it stems from the perceived social tensions of the day.

With the Merchant we are more abruptly brought to face the new world. The man keeps his trade secrets to himself, essential in a competitive business. We are given a disturbingly distanced view; the externals — the expensive hat and boots, the well-trimmed beard — point to prosperity, but what we are given are the qualities necessary for this success: financial shrewdness and the capacity to hold his cards close to his chest:

> Ther wiste no wight that he was in dette,
> So estatly was he of his governaunce
> With his bargaynes and with his chevyssaunce.

(ll.280–282)

Again there is the self-assertion which depends on doing others down. The Merchant is, of course, a wealth-creator, and as such is sharply contrasted with the next pilgrim who, for all his qualities of learning, is essentially a financial parasite. The Clerk of Oxford depends on what 'he myghte of his freendes hente' (l.299). As a wealthy man the Merchant does not expose himself to physical risk. Just as those in positions of power in the country employ others to protect their hunting, so the real face of his business is revealed not in his prosperity but in the attitude of the agent of his class, the Shipman. Nine lines of the portrait of the Shipman (ll.401–409) are certainly a record of enormous competence and experience as a navigator, but his function as a competitor is starkly brought out in the assumption that human values, 'nyce conscience' (l.398), do not matter, and that violent death is the normal outcome of coming off second best in what was essentially a commercial rivalry.

The more the commercial world comes to the fore in the *General Prologue* the more sinister and uncompromising the portraits become. Even the character who orders the framework of the tales, the Host, reveals that his good humour always depends on his being paid. Enjoyment comes when the bills have been settled:

> And spak of myrthe amonges othere thynges,
> Whan that we hadde maad oure rekenynges
>
> (ll.759–760)

Payment continually features in his speech. The prize for the best tale will be 'a soper at oure aller cost' (l.799) but this cost will be paid to the Host, who will provide the meal. The generosity is not at his own expense. And there is no pleasant system of forfeits proposed for anyone who drops out of the tale-telling game or who breaks the rules. It is twice stressed what the punishment will be:

> And whoso wole my juggement withseye
> Shul paye al that we spenden by the weye
>
> (ll.805–806)

and

> Whoso be rebel to my juggement
> Shal paye for al that by the wey is spent.
>
> (ll.833–834)

The potential fine is enormous, quite enough to keep everyone in order. In the light of this, the Host's reassurance to the pilgrims that he will accompany them 'Right at myn owene cost' (l.804) appears as an investment just as much as the promptings of generosity. The statement also raises the question of why the Host needed to state this: what would the pilgrims normally expect of such a man?

Of course the practical business sense of the Host cannot be put forward as overwhelming evidence of an increasingly vicious and mercantile society, but it is revealing to look at the most heated exchange the Host becomes involved in. At the end of his tale the Pardoner invites all the pilgrims to pay him for the opportunity to see and touch his bogus relics. The Host rounds on the Pardoner with such vigorous crudity that it takes the Knight to restore calm. It is no accident that it is between the Host and the Pardoner that this vitriolic hostility is found. While there are other predators present, it is the Pardoner who presents a direct threat to the Host's call on the purses of all the pilgrims. The Friar and the Summoner compete for a more limited market. Anyone who attends church is a potential source of revenue to the Pardoner. It is significant that he is the only pilgrim at whose portrait we are encouraged to laugh:

> Hym thoughte he rood al of the newe jet
>
> (1.682)

— but while that may have seemed the case to him, we are prompted to see that he is wrong. In the same way the ambiguity about his sexuality, 'a geldyng or a mare' (1.691) seems an attempt at disarming the threat he poses.

This concentration of aggression in the characters and characteristics centrally involved with the financial world and hence the political structure of late fourteenth century England shows how the portraits grow from their society. However virtuous you may be, your virtue cannot be isolated from your standing in financial terms. Even the Plowman's exemplary qualities are expressed as supportive of a particular economic system:

> His tithes payde he ful faire and wel,
> Bothe of his propre swynk and his catel.
>
> (ll.539–540)

Foreign trade was a major economic element in the wealth of the country. While the internal tensions had only recently broken out into an open rising in 1381, a few years later Chaucer gives us in the Shipman a chilling insight into the bottom line of all the dealing and bartering: the Merchant's 'Flaundryssh bever hat' (1.272), the expensive livery of the Guildsmen, indeed all the prosperity and potential prosperity, rely ultimately on the efficiency and readiness of the Shipman's knife.

AFTERTHOUGHTS

1

What distinctions does Spencer Ellis draw in this essay between different kinds of detail?

2

Do you agree that there are 'virtually no moments in the *General Prologue* when we can be certain that overt criticism of a character is clearly implied in the text' (page 55)?

3

What importance does Spencer Ellis attach to economic and commercial factors in the *General Prologue*?

4

Can the *General Prologue* usefully be read by someone with no knowledge of fourteenth-century England?

Angus Alton

*Angus Alton was Head of English at
Davies's College, London, and is
currently researching for the Southern
Examining Group.*

ESSAY

Chaucer's two 'corages': moral balance in the *General Prologue*

One of the major problems in understanding the *General
Prologue* or one of the various tales that follow it — assuming,
that is, that one has bridged the language barrier — is that one
is studying what is essentially only part of a text. It is akin to
studying, say, Act III of *Hamlet* or the opening Phase of *Tess
of the D'Urbervilles*; only the problem is worse in that the
obvious solution to the other cases — reading the rest of the text
— is neither practicable nor ultimately possible for *The Canterbury Tales*. First, even as it stands, it really is an enormous
work, and that means an awful lot of background reading, even
in translation. And secondly, of course, the work is unfinished:
so judgement of context can be provisional at best.

To be fair, it must be admitted that each tale and the *General
Prologue* can be studied as self-contained texts. They are both
rich enough and internally coherent enough to provide ample
interest. What is more, no doubt most teachers do try to provide
their students with a variety of useful contextual information.
You may look at, or be told about, the juxtaposed tales for
example; or there may be mention that the text you are looking

at forms part of some greater whole, some particular theme that has been seen as common to many of the tales, such as the marriage debate. Most likely of all if you are studying one of the tales, you will look at the description of the story-teller in the *General Prologue*. (In fact, this habit is recognised in most editions of the single tales where they provide the relevant extract.)

But this way of glancing at the *General Prologue* brings into focus one of the odder aspects of the study of this introductory poem. The examination of the *General Prologue* often concentrates on the portraits of the pilgrims and ignores many of the factors in the work which, I would argue, profoundly affect our understanding of the material in those portraits. The text is read as little more than a series of portraits-in-words or sometimes as a sort of history book — a look at medieval life — rather than as a literary work. Quite apart from the fact that such a reading suggests to me a rather odd impression of Chaucer sitting down to provide posterity with a glimpse into his society (and which author's chosen readership is ever directly and more or less exclusively posterity?) it also ignores what for me is one of the advantages of the *General Prologue* over any of the tales. The work *is* a prologue and, as such, may be expected to offer some insight into the central themes and preoccupations of the whole work, just as the Prelude does for *Middlemarch*.

In fact, the more one thinks about it the more limited and limiting such an approach becomes. Quite simply, it misses out so much. For a start, it fails to take into account the fact that the poem is essentially a dramatic monologue: it presents us with, not the author's own perceptions, but those of a participant in the pilgrimage. And Chaucer the pilgrim is no more to be considered reliable than Gulliver in *Gulliver's Travels*, or Lockwood in *Wuthering Heights*. However, this aspect of the *General Prologue* is dealt with elsewhere in this volume; I wish to focus here on a rather different issue that the over-concentration on the portraits tends to overlook. As I mentioned above, we might expect the prologue to a work to provide us with some idea of the kind of themes we are to encounter in the main body of that text, and my argument is that this is precisely what happens with the *General Prologue*.

Indeed, it becomes immediately apparent that, while the individual portraits make up the bulk of the poem, they form neither the whole of it, nor surely the most significant section. The first 42 lines of the poem are concerned with the setting and from line 715 to the end — apart from the description of the Host — provide an account of the events of the pilgrims' first night on the road, as they gather at the Tabard. It is something of a truism that the opening and closing sections of a text, even an essay, should provide the essential skeleton of the work, while the central portion contains the meat. After all, one of my contentions is that this is true for *The Canterbury Tales* as a whole and that, since we don't have the ending, we must look for clues in the beginning; all we are doing now is applying that same principle to the *General Prologue*.

When we do, all sorts of interesting questions start to arise. For example, Chaucer concludes his series of portraits by suggesting that he has told us:

> . . . in a clause,
> Th'estaat, th'array, the nombre, and eek the cause
> Why that assembled was this compaignye.

(ll.715–717)

This wonderfully simple sounding claim is, as is typical with Chaucer, by no means as straightforward as it appears. Yes, we know the condition, the rank, of the various pilgrims; yes, the clothing; yes, the number; but what exactly have we learnt about the cause of this company's coming together? The obvious answer to this — and perhaps the one that the narrator himself would provide — is that they have assembled for the holy purpose of pilgrimage. But such an answer clearly won't do. One of the most easily agreed factors in the ironic effects of the *General Prologue* is that few of the pilgrims are holy, and thus we need to consider the kind of motivation that might be the 'cause' for the presence of each pilgrim.

We need, in fact, to look more deeply, and to do this with any kind of efficiency we need first to equip ourselves with the kind of parameters and criteria that are active within the work. Where better to start with this task than the beginning? For surely we are immediately confronted with a surprise, with something that suggests that any preconceptions we may have

C

about a work entitled *The Canterbury Tales*, and, indeed, about the quality of medieval life in general, need to be revised. The poem is set in April, to be sure; that is, it is Easter, and the traditional time for pilgrimage. But far from emphasising the lenten and renunciatory aspect of the run up to Easter, the poem begins with its justly famous celebration of the joys of spring. The language is highly sensual, often sexual; the references to the Ram and Zephirus are pagan, astrological and mythological. Of course, the medieval Church had become adept at tolerating such references while maintaining a disapproving stance, but it is hard to see quite how such a thoroughly secular opening can be reconciled in any simple way with a religious impulse.

We are, in short, already required to respond to irony, well before the supposedly un-ironic description of the Knight; and there is one particular aspect of this irony which is especially helpful for our wider understanding of what is going on in the poem. This occurs at the precise moment at which the idea of pilgrimage is introduced: when, we are told:

> . . . smale foweles maken melodye,
> That slepen al the nyght with open ye
> (So priketh hem nature in hir corages)
> Thanne longen folk to goon on pilgrimages

(ll.9–12)

'Corage' here is usually glossed as 'heart', but that does not seem to me to be a very helpful translation; *The Riverside Chaucer* Glossary, among several meanings for the word includes 'desire', and certainly such an idea conveys much more of what is being described here. Nature is stimulating the nightingales' instincts or animal spirits, and thus causing them to stay awake all night in pursuit of a mate. Whatever specific gloss one attaches to 'corage' here, the idea is clear, and it is one which immediately provides some sort of answer to the question of cause for pilgrimage. It is easy to believe, for example, that the Wife of Bath is also responding to a mating instinct: she is later to tell us that she would welcome a sixth husband, and a pilgrimage is a wonderful opportunity for scouting. (It is worth noting, in this context, that she has been to five different destinations on previous pilgrimages, and has been married five times.) At the very least, the journey offers opportunities for further 'wandrynge by the weye' (l.467). By the same token: the Squire actually imitates the nightingale:

> So hoote he lovede that by nyghtertale
> He sleep namoore than dooth a nyghtyngale.

(ll.97–98)

It is hard not to make assumptions about what a character of such natural exuberance is doing on the pilgrimage.

But assumptions are dangerous things, and our perception of the issue is added to by the recurrence of the corage/pilgrimage rhyme within ten lines of its first use. This time Chaucer is telling us about himself:

> In Southwerk at the Tabard as I lay
> Redy to wenden on my pilgrymage
> To Caunterbury with ful devout corage

(ll.20–22)

Here again the gloss of 'heart' is rather misleading: at the very least it obscures the major difference in implications between the word in its two contexts. I prefer something like 'spirit', partly because it contrasts vividly with my suggested 'animal spirits' for the first use. The point, however, is not to get tied down with disputes about translation, but to investigate the implications of this striking repetition. At one level, for instance, it may cause us to think about the self-knowledge of the narrator. Can we really accept at this moment that he is fully devout, given the tone of the opening twenty lines in general, and the other meaning of 'corage' in particular? Doubts about this may help to explain his failure to take issue with the Monk's less than monastic attitude ('I seyde his opinion was good' — l.183) or the way he seems to overlook the merits of the Nun's Priest, which suggests he is dazzled by the Prioress herself. Certainly, the amount of physical description of the Prioress implies some very close observation.

There is, too, a much wider set of implications that these two uses of 'corage' so close together opens up; and it is these implications that I wish chiefly to concentrate on. To understand the two aspects of the word — corresponding as they do to the spiritual and secular aspects of human existence — brings to the fore in our reading of the poem the main question: what are we to make of the various specific or single insights we acquire? That is, what results from the doubts we may have about the self-knowledge of the narrator, discussed above, and, more generally, what arises from the doubts we have about most of the pilgrims? In what terms are we to express these doubts?

In a sense, the answer to these questions is implicit in the very presence of that sensual opening passage and in the exploitation of the ambiguity in 'corage'. We are being warned from the outset not to oversimplify, and not to make assumptions. Judgement is a very problematic issue and our tendency to base some of our opinions on prejudice and on inadequate evidence needs to be checked. Instead we need tolerance and caution whenever we start to arrive at conclusions, which, moreover, must always be readily revised.

Thus the main body of the *General Prologue* provides frequent opportunities for us to exercise the twin qualities of tolerance and caution. An interesting aspect of this arises from the nature of irony itself. Because we are involved in the process of understanding much more actively when we understand through irony, it is all too easy to become rather self-congratulatory at having seen the meaning beneath the surface: our search for interpretation stops at that point, especially if what we have deduced seems to involve exposing some major character flaw, such as hypocrisy. But this is unwise, as a consideration of what we learn about two of the prime hypocrites will show. Smugly we detect the implications of what we are told: we are suspicious of the causes of the 'ful many a mariage' that the Friar has made 'at his owene cost' (ll.212–213) and we wonder quite how 'hoot' is the Pardoner's 'walet . . ./ Bretful of pardoun' (ll.686–687). But so busy are we detecting abuses of religious authority and laughing at the Pardoner's effeminacy that we forget to think carefully about *all* that we learn. We forget, for example, that both are likely to be skilful story-tellers: their survival as rogues depends upon that, and we should not be surprised that the Pardoner's story is almost successful enough to make his audience forget that they have been told that his relics are false. More importantly, their very success as story-tellers means that the joke of their hypocrisy is ultimately on them. Those they convince by their preaching, those they excite to genuine repentance, are saved. Significantly, we are told that the Friar is able to preach a 'ferthyng' out of even the poorest widow (ll.252–255) and we are surely reminded of Christ's parable of the widow's mite, which is worth more in God's eyes than vast sums from wealthy men.

What is called for, then, is thoroughly careful, and as far as possible, unselective reading. Of course, in some cases even close attention won't help. No amount of thought will give us much of a clue to the character of the Nun's Priest, nor to the likely quality of his tale — although it is possible in this case to detect some suggestion of resentment of his being over-shadowed by his employer: that is, even here, careful thought can provide some clues. Even more strikingly, the Monk is a character we all find fairly easy to assess, yet it is clear from the reactions to his tale that we are not the only ones to be surprised that his tale does not reflect our assumptions about his easy worldliness.

This is perhaps the ultimate message about the need for caution in forming judgements: the information we are provided with is in some way misleading: and such caution is clearly required when it comes to the seemingly virtuous characters on the pilgrimage. Quite apart from Terry Jones's fine critique in *Chaucer's Knight* (London, 1985), one question needs to be asked about all the good figures on the pilgrimage. After all, surely it is easy to offer an explanation of the 'cause' for their presence: an opportunity for some quiet religious contemplation, followed by worship at the shrine of the 'hooly blisful martir' (l.17). But why, then, does no one raise any objection to the Host's suggestion of the story-telling competition? It is important, in this context, to consider the terms of the competition and the prize to be awarded. The prize is a thoroughly earth-bound one — a free supper clearly places the needs of the body at the forefront of our regard — and it is especially worldly when one considers how Harry Bailly stands to profit from his decision, for the meal is to be consumed at his own inn. What is more, no reservations about the proposal are expressed, even by the Parson, whose other-worldliness is so emphasised when he is described to us; in a way, more importantly, no one reading the poem is likely to be surprised or worried by this, for, by this stage, Chaucer's skill has done its work and we almost approve such an unspiritual attitude.

This is especially so when we take into account the criteria that Harry Bailly suggests as being appropriate for the competition. The winner will be the one who tells 'Tales of best sentence and moost solaas' (I.798). Such criteria echo the two sides to 'corage' that the *General Prologue* began with: instruction needs to be entertaining, and the best entertainment is instructive; true 'corage' is that which recognises and balances the secular, animal side of our nature, but does not neglect the spiritual. The Clerk epitomises the failure of one dimension, neglecting the animal side (his horse, as well as he himself suffers for this, being 'As leene . . . as is a rake' — I.287) and, it seems, capable of talking only of 'hy sentence' (I.306) without the necessary 'solaas'. At the other end of the scale we may think of the Merchant whose conversation is similarly dull:

> His resons he spak ful solempnely,
> Sownynge alwey th'encrees of his wynnyng.

> (ll.274–275)

He manages to combine worldly concerns with pomposity: an unattractive compound.

Perhaps the most important result of including the perceptions offered by the opening and closing sections of the *General Prologue* is that they reinforce most of our responses to the individual portraits. Neither the excessive plainness of the Parson nor the excessive gourmandising of the Franklin is evidence of a soul in harmony. Of course, the Wife of Bath or the Miller haven't got it right either — but there is a richness to their experience which suggests that they, and those like them, are by no means unwelcome figures to Chaucer. The poem is a celebration of human complexity and human variety, and Chaucer, whose concept of heart, of 'corage' includes both the impulses which drive the nightingales and those which inspire devotion, would surely join with Wordsworth in offering:

> Thanks to the human heart by which we live,
> Thanks to its tenderness, its joys, and fears.

> (Ode on 'Intimations of Immortality')

AFTERTHOUGHTS

1

What two 'corages' are identified by Alton? Explain their significance to the argument of this essay.

2

To what extent does a reading of the *General Prologue* demand 'twin qualities of tolerance and caution' (page 68)?

3

How can one recognise irony?

4

What ambiguity does Alton highlight regarding the terms of the story-telling competition (pages 69–70), and how does this relate to his argument?

Claire Saunders

Claire Saunders teaches English at Lavant House, and is an experienced A-level examiner.

ESSAY

Chaucer's art of portraiture: subject, author and reader

Portraiture has two obvious components — the person who sits for the portrait and the artist who paints it; in terms of literature, these are the subject and the author of a portrait. But there is also a third component — viewer, or reader. Although for many portraits, whether painted or written, this third component can seem irrelevant, this is not usually the case in the *General Prologue* to *The Canterbury Tales*. In the essay which follows I intend to look at a range of Chaucer's portraits, showing how subject, author and reader interact with varying degrees of subtlety.

Perhaps the simplest sort of portrait is the snapshot: it is unplanned, lacking in technical style and exists only as a record of its subject. Chaucer's Yeoman strikes me as similar to a typical snapshot. The portrait is full of exact detail. There is the Yeoman's physical appearance ('a not-heed' and 'a broun visage'), his clothing ('cote and hood of grene') complete with accessories ('belt' and 'bawdryk' and 'gay bracer'), his equipment ('a swerd and a bokeler', a 'gay daggere', 'An horn', 'A sheef of pecok arwes') and even his personal talisman, the 'Cristofer'. The details add up to a bright and complete whole but they seem to be expressed at random, the somewhat uninspired vocabulary and the jerky sentence structure giving the impression of a clumsy list:

> Upon his arm he baar a gay bracer,
> And by his syde a swerd and a bokeler,
> And on that oother syde a gay daggere
>
> . . .
>
> An horn he bar, the bawdryk was of grene;
> A forster was he, soothly, as I gesse.

(ll.111–117)

As a portrait it is superficial, satisfying only to someone interested in feudalism or forestry (or to the subject himself, if he ever existed).

Taking the subject of a portrait as its major component has formed the basis of many studies of the *General Prologue*, the pilgrims being sorted into sets according to social status, profession, morality or appearance. Chaucer himself seems to encourage this tendency to view his portraits as contemporary snapshots when he describes his task as:

> To telle yow al the condicioun
> Of ech of hem, so as it semed me,
> And whiche they weren, and of what degree,
> And eek in what array that they were inne

(ll.38–41)

But he is speaking here in the persona of a fellow-pilgrim, in order to exploit an apparently direct and first-hand viewpoint: Chaucer on-the-spot, a sort of journalist. The real Chaucer is the author who created both this persona and the pilgrims, the majority of whom are presented not as journalistic snapshots but as carefully drafted portraits. The craft lies in the adaptation of descriptive techniques to fit the particular purpose of each separate portrait.

In some cases Chaucer's purpose is to praise a certain standard of human behaviour and his technique is idealisation — the subject being selected, or rather created, as a pattern to be followed. Chaucer's Parson is a good example of idealisation. The author's purpose is clear, dominating from the introductory 'A good man was ther of religioun' (l.477) to the summarising 'A bettre preest I trowe that nowher noon ys' (l.524). There seems to be a single-minded objectivity in Chaucer's approach; he makes no personal comment other than the conventional 'I trowe' in the line just quoted. All the details of the Parson's actions and attitudes conform to a perfect stereotype. At the heart of the portrait is a single image, that of the Gospel's Good Shepherd, an archetypal image which gives concrete form to the abstraction which is conveyed in the accumulating adjectives — 'good', 'hooly', 'benygne', 'diligent', 'pacient', 'vertuous' and so on. The Parson is pictured striding the English countryside, 'in his hand a staf' and his figure acquires strength from being contrasted with the medieval counterpart of the Gospel's hireling shepherd, the 'mercenarie' priest, who abandons his parishioners to 'the wolf' for the sake of a sinecure job in London. In keeping with the imagery is the language in which the Parson's attitudes are expressed:

> . . . if gold ruste, what shal iren do?
> For if a preest be foul, on whom we truste,
> No wonder is a lewed man to ruste;
> And shame it is, if a preest take keep,
> A shiten shepherde and a clene sheep.

(ll.500–504)

The balanced structure, the paired opposites ('gold'/'iren', 'preest'/'lewed', 'shiten'/'clene') and the down-to-earth vocabulary all have a biblical simplicity and directness. Unlike the quirky, murky portraits of the other pilgrims whose professions in some way overlap his, the Parson's is a pure, distilled portrait, limpidly presented, befitting an ideal which is offered as a pattern of living. A similar combination of purpose and technique is evident in the Plowman, the lay counterpart of his brother and Chaucer's other idealised portrait.

The Summoner represents a diametrically opposite form of portraiture, the caricature. Here the author's purpose is to present an absolute of how *not* to be and the caricature form is, like the idealisation, designed didactically as a way of conveying a strong, simple impression. In the case of the Summoner the details — of feature, diet, attitudes, life-style — are subservient to a single dominant idea, all concentrated in the central image of hell-fire. The 'ercedekenes curs' (l.655) which the Summoner sneeringly dismisses is more or less a declaration of damnation, a point which Chaucer underlines by making his only direct, unequivocal comment in the whole of the *General Prologue*:

> Of cursyng oghte ech gilty man him drede,
> For curs wol slee right as assoillyng savith

'Assoillyng', translated as 'absolution', suggests the cleansing, cooling process which is exactly what the Summoner himself needs, not only spiritually but also physically. The hot, intemperate components of his diet ('garleek, oynons, and eek lekes,/ ... strong wyn, reed as blood' — ll.634–635) are paralleled by — perhaps they cause — his hot, intemperate behaviour, and are reflected in his physiognomy:

> ... a fyr-reed cherubynnes face,
> For sawcefleem he was, with eyen narwe.
> ...
> With scalled browes blake and piled berd.

> (ll.624–627)

Even the medicaments to which the Summoner resorts are burning corrosives, not soothing lotions. Chaucer's condemnation of the Summoner is total but, although he presents a devil — enough to terrify children — this is a cartoon devil, a sort of gargoyle, perhaps. The Summoner's ludicrous accessories (a 'gerland' and a 'bokeleer ... maad ... of a cake') make him a figure to ridicule. Chaucer's purpose is similar in the Pardoner and results in another caricature, a portrait which inspires both scorn and disgust.

But the majority of portraits in the *General Prologue* are neither as unfocused as that of the Yeoman nor as firmly manipulated as that of the Parson and the Summoner. Most result from a careful balance between the demands of the subject and those of the author; the pilgrims seem to stand as individual representatives of certain human types, the subject being used to express the author's vision. At first glance the Wife of Bath portrait exists simply to celebrate its subject, the author apparently reduced to the role of dumbfounded recorder as he describes the stockings 'of fyn scarlet reed', the shoes 'ful moyste and newe', the 'hipes large' and the 'spores sharpe' — everything proclaiming the Wife of Bath's self-confident, extrovert personality. But Chaucer's voice is an essential element. His

'and that was scathe' response to the revelation that the Wife
was 'somdel deef' (l.447) immediately establishes him in the role
of slightly nosey supporter and the 'I dorste swere' affirmation
of the magnificent head-gear (ll.453–454) suggests a breathless
sort of partisanship. After mentioning, apparently casually, the
'oother compaignye in youthe' that preceded the five husbands,
Chaucer rushes in with 'But therof nedeth nat to speke as
nouthe' (ll.461–462), ostentatiously slamming the door in the
face of the gawping listener — *we* are not allowed to hear,
apparently. With Chaucer's interpreting presence the Wife of
Bath is a marvellously humorous portrait.

The comical persona of Chaucer — the innocent,
impressionable, inoffensive fellow-pilgrim — is a key element
in the technique of Chaucer the author. His presence is discreet
in the extreme, but very productive. The Guildsmen, for
instance, seem determined to pose for the most impressive of
group portraits. They appear:

<blockquote>
alle in o lyveree,
Of a solempne and a greet fraternitee.
</blockquote>

(ll.363–364)

Their accessories are carefully chosen and ostentatiously
displayed — everything to emphasise the civic dignity of those
destined to be aldermen. But then Chaucer, apparently having
gained some extra information — the 'human angle' of the journalist — introduces the men's wives:

<blockquote>
And eek hir wyves wolde it wel assente;
It is ful fair to been ycleped 'madame,'
And goon to vigilies al bifore,
And have a mantel roialliche ybore.
</blockquote>

(ll.374–378)

Instantly the whole pompous charade collapses as the
Guildsmen are visualised in their domestic setting, hen-pecked
by their snobbish womenfolk. Chaucer appears ingenuous —
'And elles certeyn were they to blame' (l.375) — but his revelation has been devastating.

A more blatant and significant intrusion of Chaucer-the-
participating-pilgrim, used to provide an extra dimension for

Chaucer-the-portraitist, is seen in the portrayal of the Monk. Here the physical and biographical details all support the powerful (if somewhat ambiguous) designation of the Monk as 'A manly man, to been an abbot able'(l.167). The portrait then moves into reporting the Monk's modern attitudes to the monastic vocation: he 'heeld after the newe world the space' (l.176), arguing that the world could not be served by making a monk 'Upon a book in cloystre alwey to poure' (l.185). In the middle of this exposition of the Monk's views, Chaucer says 'And I seyde his opinion was good' (l.183). Why does he say this when everything that he writes on religious practice makes it clear that Chaucer does *not* agree with the Monk? It is a dramatic device. By inserting himself as fellow-traveller, Chaucer immediately makes the Monk come to life within the form of a dialogue — or rather a monologue, as Geoffrey Chaucer is clearly playing a subordinate role. The reported speech slips effortlessly into direct speech, and the Monk is revealed in the hectoring tones of his complacent self-justification. He exaggerates ('. . . studie and make hymselven wood,/ Upon a book in cloystre alwey to poure'), he heaps up the rhetorical questions ('What sholde he studie?. . .How shal the world be served?') and finishes with the flourish of a facile defiance — 'Lat Austyn have his swynk to hym reserved!' (ll.184–187). The Monk doesn't look like a 'forpyned goost' but the sort of pride he has demonstrated qualifies him for a spell of suffering in purgatory, if not hell. Chaucer's apparently timid voice of support has been triumphantly effective in persuading the suave Monk to reveal his true nature — coarse and selfish.

One feels that a similarly self-effacing dramatic pose on the part of Chaucer in the description of the Friar must be what induces Chaucer's subject to be so eloquent in explaining the corrupt reality of, 'Ful swetely herde he confessioun':

> He was an esy man to yeve penaunce,
> Ther as he wiste to have a good pitaunce.
>
> . . .
>
> For if he yaf, he dorste make avaunt,
> He wiste that a man was repentaunt
>
> (ll.221–228)

Here the Friar's own exclamation, 'he dorste make avaunt',

captures exactly the smooth smugness which is at the heart of the Friar's profession.

As a device of portraiture Chaucer's own presence within some of the portraits — the prodding, encouraging fellow-pilgrim — is only effective in conjunction with a cooperative reader. The reader needs to be aware of the Chaucer persona in order to enter into a sort of sympathetic conspiracy with him, an alliance in getting to the truth of the subject. Chaucer's most celebrated technique of portraiture, the use of irony, is similarly dependent on the reader. Irony, based on a discrepancy or gap between what is stated and what is actually intended, needs an alert, informed reader who can spot the discrepancy, fill the gap, and thus appreciate the true import of the ironic comment.

Chaucer's portrait of the Prioress is a masterpiece of irony. He gives a minutely detailed catalogue of the Prioress's features, clothes, manners and attitudes, every item being expressed in a tone of apparent admiration. At first the Prioress's behaviour is lavishly praised, with a profusion of adverbs: 'Ful weel she soong', 'ful faire and fetisly', 'wel ytaught', 'Wel coude she carie...and wel kepe', 'Ful semely ... she raughte' (ll.122–136). The phrases are piled on top of each other in a crescendo of respectful appreciation:

> And sikerly she was of greet desport,
> And ful plesaunt, and amyable ...

(ll.137–138)

'And ... and ... And ...'. It all builds up to a crucial 'But'. The reader is suddenly pulled up: 'But, for to speken of hir conscience' (l.142). Yes — after all — this, the deeper, side to her character must be the pinnacle of this figure's perfection: 'She was so charitable and so pitous' that ...? She cried when little animals got hurt! It is total bathos. The summarising 'And al was conscience and tendre herte' is completely invalidated as it becomes evident that the Prioress's life is limited to trivialities. Then the whole catalogue slips into place as every little vanity is exposed. The reader relishes the self-conscious table-manners and every romantic detail of the Prioress's image, culminating in the gentle ambiguity of the 'Amor vincit omnia' (l.162) motto. The portrait of the Prioress is revealed as a marvellous satire on both court and convent, without Chaucer making the slightest comment.

To understand and enjoy this satire readers have to be sensitive to tone. But that is not enough. Nowadays we rely heavily on editors' notes which are, thanks to the research of historians, able to supply us with crucial contemporary information — such as that broad foreheads in women were considered attractive and that nuns were anyway expected to have their foreheads concealed by their wimples. What happens to the irony when the readers lack the necessary knowledge to be able to fill up the gap which separates what the author says from what he means? Many details might go unappreciated. In the portrayal of the Clerk for instance, an explanation of the alchemical properties of the mythical Philosopher's Stone is required before we can appreciate the comment on a student of philosophy who had 'but litel gold in cofre' (l.298). In most portraits editorial information is, as here, a bonus enabling us to relish Chaucer's wit and adding depth to the characterisation.

One portrait, however, remains problematic — that of the Knight. Generations of readers have been content to see Chaucer's 'verray, parfit gentil knyght' (l.72) as equivalent to his Parson and Plowman — an invented ideal to serve as a pattern of chivalry. But if the specific details — of battles, behaviour and achievements — are read in the light of recent medieval research (most eloquently and fascinatingly coordinated by Terry Jones in *Chaucer's Knight: A Portrait of a Medieval Mercenary* (London, 1985) — then Chaucer's portrait seems, on the contrary, to present a ruthless mercenary soldier. The argument is that the more aware of Chaucer's contemporaries would have understood the significance of the specific selection of details and would have seen the portrait as sustainedly ironic. Scholarly opinion remains divided on the Knight. The portrait must stand either as an idealisation or as a satirical stereotype; it cannot be both.

Does the interpretation of the subject matter? The Knight of the portrait probably never existed as an individual person, so it is not a question of fidelity to any specific subject. The author might reasonably have expected his fourteeth-century readers or audience to understand what his portrait was saying about its subject (though praise of perfect chivalry or condemnation of imperfect chivalry would give the same message). To the modern student of literature (as opposed to history), however, the portrait is less important for what it shows of a fictional knight than for what it shows of Chaucer. The portraits in the *General Prologue* are ultimately valued not for their subjects, but for the breadth and depth of their author's understanding and the rich subtlety of his relationship with the reader.

AFTERTHOUGHTS

1

What distinction does Saunders draw between snapshots and portraits? How helpful do you find this?

2

How important is it to understand an author's purpose in writing?

3

Do you agree that 'Of cursyng oghte ech gilty man him drede' is Chaucer's 'only direct, unequivocal comment' (page 75)?

4

Do you agree with Saunders's argument in the concluding paragraph of this essay?

Paul Oliver

Paul Oliver is a member of the English Department and Director of Drama at Forest School.

ESSAY

Ambiguous icons: Chaucer's Knight, Parson and Plowman

Critics of the *General Prologue* have shown surprising confidence in their ability to detect when Chaucer is being serious, when he's being teasingly ironical, when he's giving or withholding approval and so on, despite the fact that he is the most elusive of authors and hides behind a bewildering array of disguises. Even those who are alert to the constantly changing tones of the narrator's voice have, without reservation, seen the Knight, Parson and (to a lesser degree) the Plowman as moral giants whose shadows extend over the whole *General Prologue* and beyond. The body of commentary surrounding the text has often shielded the three portraits from real, probing critical attention. Also, being taken as different versions of basically the same person has sometimes caused their virtues to be generalised and blurred their individual characteristics. One especially misleading effect of this is the notion that all three are equally motivated by religious fervour. From here it's only a short step to bending isolated details so that they fit this overall judgement — seeing, for example, the Knight's rust-stained tunic as an indication of his piety since he has not bothered to change into special pilgrimage clothes. So cut and dried a reading deprives the text of its characteristic ambiguity and also much of its bite at some of its most crucial points.

To take the Knight first: it's easy to see why readers have thought of him as 'a true hero, a good, great and wise man' (Blake's words were written in 1809 but they could easily be the verdict of a much more recent commentator). The narrator repeatedly calls the Knight 'worthy' (ll.43, 47, 50, 64 and 68) and by way of explanation we're shown that he is both dedicated to the ideals traditionally associated with knighthood and a man of action at the same time: his military record certainly sounds impressive. Then there's no denying that his personal qualities (or those that are mentioned) contrast favourably with those of other pilgrims: he is said to be meek (l.69) where others are brashly assertive or quietly self-seeking. Indeed, he has never spoken 'vileynye' to a soul (ll.70–71), an important distinction when so many pilgrims are proved by their own words to be either fraudulent or pretentious. As far as we can tell, he isn't attempting to cut a particular sort of figure: he is not trying to appear courtly (like the Prioress) or fashionable (like the Pardoner) or even wealthy (like the Merchant). But do these details of praiseworthy behaviour and unblemished character in fact constitute a picture of perfection?

In his controversial book *Chaucer's Knight* (London, 1985), Terry Jones answers this key question by arguing that since the Knight's battles were either dismal failures or bloody mass-acres, the Knight has little to be proud of, and is in any case clearly an example of the new brand of mercenary making itself felt in medieval Europe. But it's bold to conclude from this that the Knight is at the very centre of Chaucer's satire. We are on very dangerous ground indeed when we start evaluating four-teenth-century texts in the light of twentieth-century liberal sensibilities. If we take the view that Chaucer must have disapproved of the Knight's activities because he must have been a pacifist (being basically a decent sort), we're imposing our own perceptions on Chaucer, distorting his text and, inci-dentally, implying that what Chaucer thought is the critical issue! The Knight may well have been engaged in bloodshed, but there is nothing to indicate that either he or his creator would see this as contradicting the chivalric code embedded in the Knight's portrayal. Indeed, since the code entailed fighting for your country, it could be said to have necessitated attempting to kill the enemy.

It's a help to remember that the *General Prologue* never suggests that the pilgrims are wrong in their own private estimate of themselves. The Prioress, for example, thinks of herself as a fine lady and does not pretend to be a model nun; the Monk, far from deluding himself that he's a paragon of monkish virtue, openly questions the rules of his order; however much the Pardoner deceives his audiences, he does not deceive himself about the authenticity of his relics or the altruism of his motives. And so with the Knight. When Chaucer says of him that 'he loved chivalrie,/ Trouthe and honour, fredom and curteisie' (ll.45–46), there is no need to doubt it. The issue is not whether he really does pursue these aims but whether he is right to — whether, in other words, these are appropriate virtues to celebrate in the context of the late fourteenth century (and in the context of a religious pilgrimage). In the same way we ask ourselves whether the Prioress's courtliness, harmless though it appears to be, is of the slightest relevance to herself or others.

Actually there is nothing new in noting that the Knight is out of tune with his times. Many readers have sensed that the Knight supports a system which is doomed, but for them this is a positive merit: their Knight is a man fighting a vigorous rearguard action in defence of traditional values in a rapidly changing world. I would argue that it's not so clear-cut. Even without resorting to the pointless claim that Chaucer himself, being deeply involved in the political and economic life of his century, must be out of sympathy with the Knight, we can see the weaknesses of an exclusively admiring response to him. Reading on from the end of the Knight's portrait shows us just how isolated a figure he is in a society dominated more and more by mercantile concerns in which traditional feudal relationships have been largely dissolved. It's too easy to fall into the trap of assuming that time-honoured ideals are necessarily the best. As the Headmaster in Alan Bennett's play *Forty Years On* says, 'Standards always are out of date. That is what makes them standards.' But what if the society which sanctioned the standards has itself moved on to a point where they have little meaning except as reminders of the past? There has to be a *context* in which they can operate. *The Knight's Tale* and its reception indicate that the Knight is accorded the respect, and also the slightly amused tolerance, reserved for those we recognise as embodying a sophisticated but outmoded philosophy. When he is describing the entry into Athens of the two rivals Palamon and Arcite who are going to take their armies into the lists to battle it out, the Knight pauses to address his fellow-pilgrims in order to express his approval:

> For if ther fille tomorwe swich a cas,
> Ye knowen wel that every lusty knyght
> That loveth paramours and hath his myght,
> Were it in Engelond or elleswhere,
> They wolde, hir thankes, wilnen to be there —
> To fighte for a lady, benedicitee!
> It were a lusty sighte for to see.

(I, ll.2110–2116)

(If such a situation arose tomorrow, you well know that every active knight who loves passionately and possesses the strength would, both in England and elsewhere, wholeheartedly wish to be there — to fight for a lady, God bless us! It would be a pleasant sight to see!) Coming as this outburst does in the middle of a story which contains suffering and bloodshed on an epic scale, it confirms our impression of the Knight's naïvety: he makes here an assumption which his listeners do not share. They, of course, are too polite to say anything, but it's interesting that when the tale is over, instead of specific mention being made of details of its content, as is the case with the following two tales, everyone agrees that it is a 'noble storie' (I, l.3111) and then they hurry on to the question of who should tell the next tale. There's a silent conspiracy among the pilgrims not to engage with the Knight's words and values on more than a superficial level. They're thus kept at a safe distance.

One other key phrase from the Knight's description in the *General Prologue* deserves close scrutiny. In line 62 we're told that he had 'foughten for oure feith at Tramyssene'. It's perhaps the remark that more than any other has encouraged readers to link the Knight with the Parson. His other alleged attributes, though, diminish the importance of this isolated statement. Take, once again, lines 45–46: whatever the exact meaning of 'chivalrie', it would take considerable ingenuity to give it a religious reference; 'honour', admittedly an even trickier word to pin down, hardly promotes the idea that the Knight's basic motivation is the Christian faith. However praiseworthy it is to protect someone else's 'honour', if you're really pursuing your own, the word hardly signifies much more than 'reverence' or 'reputation'. We know from line 50 ('And evere honoured for his worthynesse') and from the use of words such as 'degree' (1.55) and 'prys' (1.67) that his position was of central concern to him, but it does not neatly dovetail with the notion of humble Christian piety. It's really safer not to rest too much weight on a phrase like 'for oure feith', especially when we don't know exactly what charge this carried for contemporary audiences. We can say with less fear of contradiction that the portrait as a whole gives the impression of a man whose own ideals and interests are basically secular. At best lines 45–46 encourage just the ambiguous sort of response that is so much a feature of the *General Prologue*.

If we read the figure of the Knight as I suggest, we avoid forcing ourselves to see him as a bastion of high seriousness uneasily placed between the opening of the work (a passage whose comedy becomes more telling when we encounter the flesh and blood pilgrims and their actual motives) and the description of the Squire, in which the young man is compared to a meadow and a nightingale. Instead of being temporarily gagged, the narrator's ambiguous, potentially satirical tone is heard at the outset establishing what sort of document Chaucer is writing. We no longer have to resort to the ingenious but implausible explanation that the narrator gets us used to hearing pilgrims praised without reservation before turning the tables and mocking them. We may be deprived of the moral yardstick beloved of earlier critics, but do we really need the contrast with a perfect character unambiguously presented to show up the fraudulence of the Friar? If we do judge others by the Knight's standards, we apply criteria which are not so much wrong as simply irrelevant.

Reading the Knight in this way brings Chaucer's methods there more in line with what he does in other portraits. The

Parson, on the other hand, represents a radical departure from the norm. There's certainly nothing in the text that even the most morally demanding of readers could take exception to. However, there is an almost complete absence of individual colouring: we're not told his name or where he comes from; we're told nothing of his dress; there is nothing like the Shipman's knife or the Miller's hairy wart to facilitate visualisation (and it's not true that this sort of physical detail works in an exclusively comical or satirical direction, as the Franklin's purse proves). True, we are told that the Parson carries a staff when visiting parishioners but that is really a symbolic prop which ties in with the shepherd/sheep metaphor running through the central section of the description, rather than a possession of intrinsic interest like the loaf which the Summoner has personalised by carrying it about in the manner of a shield. (In any case, unlike the Summoner his loaf, the Parson is presumably not carrying his staff on the pilgrimage: it's information about the Parson, at one remove from the illusory reality of the pilgrimage.)

The Parson, then, is unfolded solely in terms of his virtues: he is good (1.477); he is holy (1.479); he is learned (1.480) in contrast to many country priests of the time. So he is not merely an exaggerated figure in the familiar *General Prologue* style whereby every pilgrim is an expert in his or her profession or trade, he is an exaggerated stereotype. This is all the more noticeable thanks to the way the Parson follows so hard on the heels of arguably the most individually visualised of Chaucer's pilgrims, the Wife of Bath (and it's a commonplace of criticism of the *General Prologue* that the order of the portraits, its system of internal comparison and contrast, is a crucial feature of the work's structure). One effect of this is to force on our attention the idealised nature of the Parson, the way he conforms to biblical and ecclesiastical notions of priestly conduct and virtue.

So much for generalities; there are two specific anomalies on the stylistic level. Firstly, after line 500, we have a passage of an untypically theoretical nature, where the camera pulls back for a moment from the pilgrim under discussion returning with a jolt at the line 'He sette nat his benefice to hyre' (1.507):

> For if a preest be foul, on whom we truste,
> No wonder is a lewed man to ruste;
> And shame it is, if a prest take keep,
> A shiten shepherde and a clene sheep.
> Wel oghte a preest ensample for to yive,
> By his clennesse, how that his sheep sholde lyve.

(ll.501–506)

In the absence of any medieval convention for indicating direct speech, it's impossible to be sure whether this passage is a continuation of the thoughts or words of the Parson contained in the phrase 'if gold ruste, what shal iren do?' (l.500) — for a medieval writer there was no awkwardness in gliding from indirect into direct speech — or else an 'intrusion' on the part of the narrator. (The 'we' of line 501 might well be taken to suggest a remark by a layman.) Whichever is the case, Chaucer does here what he does nowhere else in the *General Prologue*: he sets up a standard within an individual description to enable immediate comparison between the specific example and the ideal.[1] The effect here is to show that there is no difference. But in the process of blurring the distinction between the ideal and the individual, the portrait makes it hard to focus clearly on the individual.

The other unusual stylistic feature is the account of what this particular Parson did *not* do:

> He sette nat his benefice to hyre
> And leet his sheep encombred in the myre
> And ran to Londoun unto Seinte Poules
> To seken hym a chaunterie for soules,
> Or with a bretherhed to been withholde

(ll.507–511)

The problem with this section is that it runs the risk of linking bad priests with energetic movement, of injecting vitality into an essentially static picture at the wrong moment. Notice, too, that the most vivid link in the chain of the shepherd/sheep

---

[1] The closest parallel is a passage (ll.177–188) in the description of the Monk. The difference, though, is that there the satire works by means of the narrator's adoption of an easily seen through tone of naïve approval.

equation is the image of the sheep left helplessly stuck in the mud by the bad shepherd/priest. Moreover, this strange use of the negative is resorted to three more times before the end of the description (at lines 516–517, 525 and 526) so that it's no exaggeration to say that, alone of all the pilgrims, the Parson is presented partly in terms of his opposite. There's a danger in all this that the reader of the *General Prologue* will come to associate liveliness with roguery and dullness with virtue. In fact it's an association that the narrator actively encourages. Take the Wife of Bath: the general consensus is that Chaucer was fascinated by this creature of his imagination. Yet her motive for coming on the pilgrimage, presumably in order to find a sixth husband if possible, must in religious terms be one of the most questionable. This is not to suggest that Chaucer himself found the virtues of his Parson in any way reprehensible, but it may be that the length of his description reflects an attempt to fulfil the duty of presenting an antidote to the vices of the Monk, Friar, Summoner and Pardoner, an attempt which had mixed results because even here presenting a picture of clerical *irresponsibility* proved an irresistible attraction. The aim critics have ascribed to Chaucer — that of getting us to admire the Parson — is badly undermined, too, by the portrait's lack of colour. How can we admire wholeheartedly what we can't visualise? How can we warm to a bundle of maxims and negatives? It's beyond the scope of this essay to establish how many priests of this type actually existed in the late fourteenth century, but it's tempting to conclude that what Chaucer was doing in the figure of the Parson was describing someone who did not in fact exist or was found so rarely as to be negligible. The description works not by showing us a good man in the company of rogues, but by juxtaposing abstract and concrete. It's only when Chaucer has finished dealing with the Parson and his equally virtuous but lacklustre brother and moves on to talking about the Miller that we feel we're back in touch with reality. (That itself is an illusion, but a successful one.)

The very feature which cuts the Parson off from the other pilgrims, his refusal to compromise with the world in which he finds himself, is unfortunately as likely to repel converts as to attract them. After all, if the Parson's parishioners are the sort of people who constitute the main body of the pilgrims, people like the Guildsmen whose chief concern is upward movement in terms of status and wealth, what are the Parson's chances of making an impact? Many of the pilgrims, wily, self-assured and knowing, would surely be more than a match for him! The narrator stresses how the Parson practises what he preaches before he preaches it, but it's hard to imagine what point of contact there could be between such a man and, say, the Shipman, of whom we are told, 'Of nyce conscience took he no keep' (1.398), a wittily understated tribute to the Shipman's ruthlessness. What we're assured of the Parson's main aim ('To drawen folk to hevene by fairnesse,/ By good ensample' — 11.519–520) sounds, like so much in the *General Prologue*, super-ficially impressive. But in the context of a gallery of pilgrims whose interests do not harmonise neatly with the Parson's, the lines have a curiously unrealistic and impotent ring. Others shine for the most part through the use they make of what they *know*: 'he/she koude' is a phrase that occurs constantly, often several times in the same description. But its only appearance in the Parson's is in the line 'He koude in litel thyng have suffisaunce' (1.490), which is another reference to his unworld-liness. Although it's meant as praise, the line shows the gulf between Parson and people. What sets him apart is his inno-cence, his quality of *not* knowing.

The Plowman, rather than the Knight, is the equivalent of the Parson in the world of work. I called him lacklustre earlier, but the word does not sufficiently take into account the fact that the portrait is so insubstantial that it is hard to characterise the man at all. His virtues are really a distillation of the Parson's — or at least some of them, especially those which refer to work. The similarity between them is pointed up by the way they are both impervious to fortune's knocks: the Parson visits his people 'in siknesse' and 'in meschief' (1.493) and the Plowman loves God 'thogh him gamed or smerte' (1.534). Also, both go beyond the call of duty in generosity, the Parson preferring giving to taking (1.487) and the Plowman working for nothing whenever he can (1.538). After the Parson we're ready for almost anything in the saintly line, but even so the phrase 'for Cristes sake' in 'He wolde thresshe, and therto dyke and delve,/ For Cristes sake, for every povre wight' (11.536–537) is surprisingly self-conscious. The *General Prologue* does not prepare us for a link between grubby-handed competence and real piety, and 'dyke and delve,/ For Cristes sake' has a distinctly jarring effect. The strain here and the lack once again of precise details about the character work against easy visualisation. The concluding remark, 'In a tabard he rood upon a mere' (1.541), is only a nod in the direction of local colouring and tells us nothing unexpected.

The Parson and Plowman are oddly connected in a manner which the text does not foreground. The Parson receives tithes; the Plowman pays them, possibly to his brother (though probably not, because the Parson, being 'a lerned man, a clerk' (1.480), is likely to have left his parents' neighbourhood and ended up in a parish further afield). The Parson is reluctant to take punitive action over the non-payment of tithes (1.486); the Plowman, poor though he is, is careful never to be in arrears ('His tithes payde he ful faire and wel' — 1.539). Why this emphasis on something which everyone was meant to do? Admittedly not everyone paid their tithes punctually (and some, as line 486 hints, withheld them). Nevertheless the remark seems to be saying what, in the context of the description as a whole, could safely have been left to be inferred. It's not an issue with any other pilgrim. Whatever the intention behind the line, its effect is to show that the two brothers are linked not only by blood but also by an economic system, even if that system is itself part of a much larger structure that would claim to be religious. However pious a man he is, the Plowman is also aware of social duties: in a society where everyone pays tithes, after all, paying them becomes a social as well as a religious duty, and lines 539–540 link the Plowman with pilgrims as diverse as the Merchant, the Manciple and the Doctor, men with whom the profit motive is paramount, but all, we may be sure, payers of tithes. The point is worth stressing because the Plowman, along with the Parson and Knight, has for too long been gazed at in too reverential a spirit as if he were in some way outside society, such separation being seen in any case as desirable.

For us as modern readers, unaware of the exact connotations of a key word such as 'worthy', it is extremely dangerous to accept what Chaucer says of his three icons at face value. To do so would be to miss not only what is there on the surface of the text but also the tensions beneath the surface, especially those created by the way English society as glimpsed in the *General Prologue* has moved on from being feudal, military and Christian (if indeed it ever was the latter, which is doubtful) to something much less homogeneous, while still retaining many vestiges of the thought and practice of earlier stages of its development. The Knight and Parson might not so much shame the other pilgrims as baffle them. There's certainly no need for us as readers to press them into service to judge their companions: their companions manage that quite adequately for themselves.

AFTERTHOUGHTS

What do you understand by 'icons'?

Do you agree that the *General Prologue* 'never suggests that the pilgrims are wrong in their own private estimate of themselves' (page 84)?

Compare Oliver's commentary on the Knight (pages 83–86) with that of Norgate (pages 11–14) and Moseley (page 114).

What arguments does Oliver put forward to suggest certain ambiguities in Chaucer's portrayal of the Parson and the Plowman?

Cedric Watts

Cedric Watts is Professor of English at Sussex University, and author of many scholarly publications.

ESSAY

Boring virtue and interesting vice: the literary conflict between morality and vitality

In this essay, Part 1 outlines a problem; Part 2 discusses the *General Prologue* to *The Canterbury Tales*, and Part 3 offers a conclusion.

1

The *General Prologue* raises very clearly one of the biggest problems perennially faced by literary critics. Repeatedly in the study of literary texts, whether by Chaucer, Shakespeare, Jonson, Pope, or dozens of other authors, the critic encounters the following paradox. Virtuous characters are often less engaging than vicious characters. Even though we may see very well that the bad characters fail various moral tests, we find that in various ways they arouse more interest and may even seem more attractive than do the relatively good ones.

This might not matter so much if it were not the case that

literary criticism is, to a large extent, a discourse of moral recommendations. Even when the critic does not purport to be a moralist, his or her writings are laden with explicit or implicit moral recommendations. When Dr Johnson, in the eighteenth century, said that 'It is always a writer's duty to make the world better',[1] his position was essentially no different from that of recent Marxist critics who condemn works which (in their view) have a right-wing tendency and commend works which (in their view) have a left-wing tendency. The discourses of politics, religion and literary criticism are all parts of the vast territory of moral discourse, in which people seek to influence other people's choices by recommending some options of conduct and disparaging others. As soon as we can communicate, we attempt to persuade. The higher a creative writer's reputation, the more the critic seeks to elicit from the writings some moral wisdom; and, given that the creative writer usually has greater prestige than the critic, the critic will usually seek to prove that the writings under consideration are so astute that they actually support his or her own outlook. If, however, the writings stubbornly refuse to be so docile, the critic may seek revenge by arguing that the writer in question has been over-estimated. The long saga of literary criticism is partly a story of human egoism: the estimation of a text's meaning and merits is so often coloured, distorted and perhaps prompted by the critic's need to find moral support in a quest to make the world more congenial to the critic. Not very many critics are able to say, 'The values of this text are totally opposed to mine, and it is a very good text'; usually, the claim is: 'This is a very good text, and if you look at it in the right way you'll see that it is sufficiently clever to support my own principles.' (One person's principles are another person's prejudices.) The critic may be led into self-contradiction, however: Dr Johnson, as I mentioned just now, said that it was always a writer's duty to make the world better; but when he looked closely at Shakespeare, the supreme British author, Johnson felt obliged to declare that 'he seems to write without any moral purpose'.[2]

---

[1] *Johnson on Shakespeare*, edited by Walter Raleigh (London, 1908; reprinted 1957), p. 21.
[2] *Johnson on Shakespeare*, pp. 20–21.

Rowland Hill, founder of the Salvation Army, 'did not see any reason why the devil should have all the good tunes';[3] in literature, the devil has many good tunes. One of the most famous critical pronouncements is William Blake's claim that Milton 'was a true Poet and of the Devil's party without knowing it'.[4] Anyone who reads *Paradise Lost* can sense what Blake meant. That epic purports to 'justify the ways of God to men'; repeatedly Milton describes the evil of Satan; yet Satan, as portrayed in the poem, elicits far stronger imaginative interest than do Milton's God and Milton's Christ. In Shakespeare's *Antony and Cleopatra*, Octavia repeatedly passes moral tests while Cleopatra repeatedly fails them; yet Octavia remains a pale pitiable figure, whereas Cleopatra engrosses our imagination. In Ben Jonson's *Volpone*, it's the vitality of Volpone himself that is fascinating, not the virtue of Bonario and Celia. In Emily Brontë's *Wuthering Heights*, the charismatic character is the brutal and vindictive Heathcliff, not the civilised Edgar Linton. Examples could be multiplied. So here's the problem: traditionally, critics have assumed that literature should offer moral sustenance, yet our experience of reading many texts gives the impression that the depiction of immorality exerts a lingering and apparently subversive fascination.

2

Chaucer's *General Prologue* to *The Canterbury Tales* provides, on a small but manageable scale, a basis for solving this problem.

There is no doubt that when he is depicting the various figures, the main terms of the depiction seem to be moral. Certainly Chaucer, like a painter, strives to give a clear visual rendition of these characters, and he specifies their careers or vocations; but it is the moral appraisal that seems mainly to

---

[3] E W Broome, *The Rev. Rowland Hill* (London, 1881)
[4] Poetry and Prose of William Blake, edited by Geoffery Keynes (London, 1927), p.182.

account for the details chosen. Within the first thirty lines we're told that these travellers have gathered for the specific purpose of a pilgrimage to Canterbury, to worship at the shrine of St Thomas: so questions underlying the assessment of the characters will naturally be 'How sincere is the piety of each of the pilgrims? Are there other motives for the journey? Are their careers, and their ways of following those careers, consistent with their ostensibly pious pilgrimage?'

As the character-descriptions are presented, we soon find that the narrator is using several sets of moral criteria for the evaluation of the characters. These sets interlink and partly overlap, but at their extremes they are in contradiction. Jesus had said, 'Ye cannot serve God and Mammon'; but medieval society, ostensibly a society devoted to service of God, was in practice often a society devoted to service of Mammon (wealth, profit, greed). The first set of criteria is the Christian set: in particular, standards of judgement suggested by the New Testament Gospels. According to this set, a person is good if he or she is pious, God-fearing and God-serving, dutiful, charitable, diligent in good works, active in helping fellow-people. The second set overlaps with the first but is not identical to it. This is the set of social criteria. According to this set, a person is good if he or she is a good neighbour, kind and helpful to fellow-people, honest, conscientious and reliable. The third set, however, takes us into a more ambiguous area. This is the set of hedonistic criteria, 'hedonistic' meaning concerned with pleasure. According to this set, a person is good if he or she is entertaining, fun to be with, amusing to hear or observe in action. The fourth set is the set of materialistic criteria (Mammon's set), according to which a person is good if he or she possesses wealth or is astute in gaining wealth. A person who is good according to sets 3 and 4 might be bad when judged by the standards of sets 1 and 2, and vice-versa. By traditional 'official' standards (dominated by the Church and the law), the sets constitute a hierarchy in which 1 is at the top and 4 is at the bottom; but by traditional 'unofficial' standards (dominated by selfish acquisitiveness) the hierarchy is, in practice, often reversed. Hence the complexity of some of the characterisations; and hence much of the famous Chaucerian irony, which can praise on the basis of set 3 or 4, while implying criticism on the basis of set 1 or 2.

D

If we were asked to select the most virtuous characters in the *Prologue*, there would be little difficulty. The term 'virtuous' strongly implies set 1 and also, somewhat less strongly, implies set 2. At the top of the list would be the Parson. He not only preaches Christianity, he exemplifies it. He's honest, humble, poor, sincere, conscientious, charitable, generous, and a helpful neighbour:

> Cristes loore and his apostles twelve
> He taughte; but first he folwed it hymselve.
>
> (ll.527–528)

Next, his brother, the Plowman: again, he's a devout Christian, and he puts his Christianity into action by working honestly and helping his neighbour:

> God loved he best with al his hoole herte
> At alle tymes, thogh him gamed or smerte,
> And thanne his neighebor right as hymselve.
>
> (ll.533–535)

Third in the list comes the Knight. Again, he's exemplary: 'A verray, parfit gentil knyght' (l.72), valiant yet 'meeke as is a mayde' (l.69), clean-living and clean-speaking. It's emphasised that for much of his career he has been a champion of Christendom, fighting infidels abroad. If I rank him lower than the Parson and the Plowman, it's only because the Christian standards invoked in their cases remind us of Christ's teachings that God looks with particular favour upon the lowly and that one should forgive enemies instead of attacking them. No doubt, in the fourteenth century, the Knight's crusading career would be regarded as admirable, and there is no flicker of hostile irony in Chaucer's depiction of him. It is simply that by the standards of set 1, the Parson and the Plowman seem likely to receive a welcome in heaven which will be even more enthusiastic than that given to the very worthy Knight; and, by the somewhat more secular standards of set 2, the Parson and Plowman have fuller credentials (as kindly helpers of their fellow-people) than he does.

The snag for us, of course, is that the Knight, the Parson and the Plowman seem such exemplary figures that they are virtually types or models of perfection. They elicit our approval rather than our interest; there's little for our imagination, or Chaucer's intelligence, to do with them. Most of the pilgrims are corrupt, in varying degrees; often they are crooked, scheming and hypocritical, or at least more worldly than (according to set 1) they should be. And it's these crooked or at least worldly characters who offer most to our imagination and intelligence. They're more fun for us as readers, as though set 3 were nearest to the set we use when we're reading fiction. Of course, the subtlest of the characters presented is undoubtedly the anonymous narrator. It is tempting to call that narrator 'Chaucer': but that would be inaccurate. *The Canterbury Tales* is an imaginative creation; and though close observation of reality has obviously contributed to the *Prologue*, there is no guarantee that any one of the characters is anything other than a fictional construct; there's no proof that Chaucer himself ever undertook such a pilgrimage with such a motley array of people; and therefore, although the narrator's views may be almost identical with Chaucer's, we should regard him as a characterisation. This narrator is obviously astutely observant, never fooled by appearances, and possesses a sharp eye for the revealing detail. He's the kind of person who can criticise privately while agreeing publicly: he sees all the hypocrisy of the Monk but yet pretends to endorse it: 'And I seyde, his opinion was good' (l.183). He provides the evidence to enable us to make hostile judgements of the conduct of many of the pilgrims: he notes the ruthlessness of the Shipman, the brutality and dishonesty of the Miller, and the hypocritical greed and avarice of the Monk, the Friar, the Manciple, the Reeve, the Summoner and the Pardoner. (He gives a strong impression that the Catholic Church was riddled with corruption.) Chaucer himself is inventing the whole scene, including that astutely observant and ironic narrator who delights in effecting collisions between those four sets of criteria that we noted just now.

One large-scale irony of the *Prologue* as a whole is that although the pilgrims — particularly since they *are* pilgrims — should serve sets 1 and 2 (the Christian and social sets), the vast majority of them are zealously serving Mammon and themselves rather than God and others. Indeed, so much worldliness, crookedness, deception and avarice is portrayed that a pious moralist might well experience disgust and dismay. Yet these are not the tones of the narrator. Often his tone is of quiet amusement; certainly not that of moral horror or scorn. Frequently, what we detect is relish: relish for the distinctiveness, the sheer and often bizarre vitality, of these rogues and hypocrites. He rises to the challenge of showing how these characters appear to themselves while showing how they appear to others. Take the worldly Monk, for instance, who loves hunting, expensive clothing and roast swan. By the standards of sets 1 and 2 he's a disgrace: a monk who's a living contradiction of the principle that monks should serve God and avoid the temptations of the flesh. His arrant hypocrisy is certainly underlined in the text:

> What sholde he studie and make hymselven wood,
> Upon a book in cloystre alwey to poure,
> Or swynken with his handes, and laboure.
> As Austyn bit? How shal the worlde be served?
> Lat Austyn have his swynk to hym reserved!

(ll.184–188)

But what emerges predominantly in this character-portrait is the sheer vitality of the Monk, his sensual gusto, his delight in the world of hunting and rich living; and, beyond that, the spectacle of worldly hedonism that he offers to the observer. Set 3 of our criteria comes into play: this Monk seems to be genial company: fun to be with. And this applies even to some of the nastier and more predatory characters: even in the case of the Summoner and the Pardoner, the narrator clearly delights in portraying their crooked ways. their outrageous tricks and hypocrisies, just as he takes pleasure in recording their bizarre and grotesque appearance. What so often makes these characters seem so credibly lifelike is the narrator's observant eye for the detail which is telling, betraying or merely outlandish. One instance is the Summoner's crazy shield ('A bokeleer hadde he maad hym of a cake' — l.668); another is the Pardoner's wild stare ('Swiche glarynge eyen hadde he as an hare' — l.684); then there are the Wife of Bath's sharp spurs, the Miller's wart with its tuft of hairs, or the disgusting 'mormal' on the Cook's shin.

What is happening, then, is that although the narrator makes us well aware of sets 1 and 2, and although he is keen to show how characters often serve sets 3 and 4 (so that ironic collisions result), he himself often seems to be governed by a further set, which relates to set 3 but goes further. 'Connoisseurship of individualism' could be its name. According to this new set, a character is good *from an artistic point of view* if that character is distinctive, curious, interesting, peculiar, bizarre. And what of Chaucer's own master-set, that set which includes the narrator's but (since it deploys and uses the narrator as a character) goes further? I suggest 'connoisseurship of life' as the name for it. It's larger than connoisseurship of individualism, because it recognises the contribution to the whole richness of life made by those characters who, by their very consistency of virtue, lack the interesting idiosyncratic complexity, the peculiarities and eccentricities, of the more worldly people. It enjoys the diversity of the moral arena and the diversity of individual appearances and life-styles; it recognises, with remarkable tolerance, the lies, trickeries and hypocrisies of the deceivers and the self-deceivers.

3

We can now return to the original problem. Why is it that in literary texts the 'bad' characters often seem to be more engaging than the 'good' characters? Part 2 has provided the basis of the answer.

When we assess a literary character, part of our assessment uses familiar moral criteria. A literary character may be a selfish and hypocritical deceiver, like the Summoner or the Pardoner. But we are never going to be victims of those particular figures, precisely because they are literary characters. They are people in quotation marks, so to speak; and our moral judgements are similarly judgements 'in quotation marks', for they apply to fictions and not to people in the street. Next, we may, like the fictional narrator of the *Prologue*, use the set of judgements termed 'connoisseurship of individualism': we may relish the particular vividness of the characterisation; and we may, like Chaucer use the set termed 'connoisseurship of life': we enjoy the vicarious knowledge of life provided by these literary instances of vitality or complexity. Morally, the Wife of

Bath is, by some obvious tests, inferior to the Plowman. But the Wife of Bath is more interesting, lively and complicated; she offers more to the imagination and to the analytic intelligence. The Prioress is, by some obvious tests, inferior to the Parson; but the Prioress, again, offers more to the imagination and to the analytic intelligence, as we follow the clues which enable us to see how her delicate sensibility and refined manners constitute a local victory for civilised conduct but a local defeat for committed Christianity: she seems to put worldly niceties first. At the same time, we can share not only the narrator's enjoyment of her comedy of manners but also Chaucer's astuteness in offering a portrait of an individual which is also an epitome of a perennial type of person — a person whose counterparts we can see around us today. In the case of the randy and twinkling-eyed Friar, we rapidly see that his lechery marks him as sinful and hypocritical by Christian standards, but he stands before us as distinctive, lively, understandable and enjoyable as a creation; part of our judgement is the literary judgement of Chaucer's artistry in imposing him so strongly and credibly on our imagination. He represents a kind of hedonistic gusto that we can observe in our world (and possibly envy), so our appreciation is a compound of ethical criticism of a character, identification of a type, and enjoyment of Chaucer's creative verve. As for the hermaphroditic Pardoner: part of us may say, 'This freak is an outrageous trickster, abusing religion and cheating the poor; a horrifying example of the corruption of the Church!'; but another part of us relishes the comedy of his brazen hypocrisy and the bizarre eccentricity of his nature and appearance; and another part of us appreciates Chaucer's skill in creating this fictional entity with such astuteness that we may understandably be tricked into assessing the Pardoner as a person rather than as a characterisation. Samuel Johnson partly solved the problem when he said: 'Imitations produce pain or pleasure, not because they are mistaken for realities, but because they bring realities to mind.'[5]

It's tempting to sum matters up by saying that when we judge literary characters, our moral judgements are largely

[5] *Johnson on Shakespeare*, p. 28.

subverted by artistic judgements. Against our sense that literature offers us an intelligent interrogation of real life, there's our
sense that literature is partly escape from real life, partly a
movement into a fantasy realm in which we can't be hurt or
robbed although we may be presented with killers and robbers.
In the case of the *Prologue* we also share, for a while, the
creative intelligence and the peculiarly humane shrewdness of
Chaucer's nature. He demonstrates to us the complexity and
confusion of the world of morality, and shows that, for a while
at least, this complexity and confusion can be enjoyed as material for comedy and connoisseurship.

While living, we habitually make moral assessments of
other people. When doing so, we often take for granted the
temporary miracle that we are alive and share the world with
an amazing diversity of living beings. The enduring words of
Chaucer, a poet who died so long ago, remind us of that brief
but recurrent miracle which encompasses and transcends our
earnest games of morality.

AFTERTHOUGHTS

1

Should literature be moral in effect?

2

'The long saga of literary criticism is partly a story of human egoism' (page 95). Do you agree with Watts's claim?

3

What do you understand by 'connoisseurship' (page 101)?

4

Do you agree that in the *General Prologue* 'moral judgements are largely subverted by aesthetic judgements (pages 102–103)?

Charles Moseley

Charles Moseley teaches English at Cambridge University and at the Leys School, Cambridge. He is the author of numerous critical studies.

ESSAY

The *General Prologue* as prologue

The Canterbury Tales is one of the most ambitious works of fiction ever conceived. Chaucer died, of course, before he could finish it or fully revise what he had written; we nevertheless have enough of it to see something of what he had in mind.

Other people had written 'frame stories' — that is, a collection of stories held together within another big story — before Chaucer. He had before him, on the one hand, the classical example of the *Metamorphoses* of Ovid; he also probably knew collections of stories and anecdotes to illustrate points in treatises on the Seven Deadly Sins (like Robert Mannyng's *Handlyng Synne*). There was also the supreme example of Boccaccio's *Decameron*, where a group of young nobles fleeing from the plague in Florence retire to a country house and amuse each other with stories. But these precedents do not come anywhere near the versatility and range of *The Canterbury Tales*.

Chaucer's revolutionary extension of the boundaries of fiction lies in two main areas: first, the telling of stories in the fictional framework of the pilgrimage to Canterbury becomes another story in its own right. The links between the tales, though in many cases only in what looks like a draft form, go far beyond anything Boccaccio had attempted and suggest that a major area of Chaucer's interest is how people respond to fiction, and how the reception of a story may be qualified by the person who tells it. Second, *The Canterbury Tales* is uniquely inclusive: within it, even as we have it, all the small narrative forms (and some not so small) of the period are represented — almost as if Chaucer was deliberately experimenting with what happened when forms normally kept distinct from each other were brought together. The long chivalric romance of *The Knight's Tale*, based on a well-shaped story set in classical times and appealing to an audience of high and noble sentiment, appears in the same collection with a parody of the down-market tail-rhyme romance, *The Tale of Sir Thopas*; it is also generically linked to the clumsy and over-ambitious romance of adventure the Squire tells. There are 'Lives of the Saints', like the tales of the Prioress and the Second Nun, and the legend of high virtue in *The Clerk's Tale* — all told in an appropriately high register of language and ornate form, the 'rime royale' stanza. There are 'confessions', very like the later form of the dramatic monologue, in the prologues of the Wife of Bath, the Pardoner, and the Canon's Yeoman; there is the ironic and very vivid verse sermon of the Pardoner and the academic prose sermon of the Parson. There are examples of romances of 'faerye', of folk-tale, of beast fable and of the *fabliau*: for there are several stories of low life, where the humour is entirely sexual or scatological (though that is not to deny more serious interests as well) — the tales of the Miller, the Reeve, the Summoner, the Friar, and the unfinished tale of the Cook. The rather old-fashioned form of the Breton *lai* makes a brief appearance in *The Franklin's Tale*. All these forms had been developed to do specific jobs, and carried with them accepted expectations and values. Nobody before had brought them together in one poem.

Chaucer's device of setting the stories within the frame of a pilgrimage elegantly allows the linking together of these different literary forms, often with contradictory functions and expectations, in a single unified whole. For pilgrimages were something most people in Chaucer's day would perform at some time or other in their lives. Very well organised, with recognised routes, inns, and places of assembly, the pilgrimage was almost the only institution in medieval society where people of different rank could mix and talk on terms of temporary intimacy; so Chaucer is able to draw representatives of all walks of life into his story in a credible group, giving to each a tale fitting — decorous — to his or her position and circumstances. (It is a delicious irony that Chaucer, writing himself into his own story as a ridiculous figure, gives himself, the acknowledged finest poet of the age, the worst verse tale — *Sir Thopas* — and when that is interrupted out of sheer boredom by the Host, a most boring prose tale.) Chaucer is playing, moreover, with a further notion of pilgrimage: contemporary works like Langland's *Piers Plowman*, or the sermons, remind us that as they travelled pilgrims often did amuse themselves by telling stories, often bawdy ones, that they were notoriously liars, and that behaviour on pilgrimages often fell far short of a decent sanctity. The Church, indeed, was uneasy about pilgrimages and their effect on pilgrims, even though they were a major source of revenue for important shrines. While some went on a pilgrimage purely out of devotion (as the Knight, Parson, Clerk and Plowman clearly do), many saw it as the medieval equivalent of the package holiday to Mallorca: an opportunity for a wild time, no questions asked when you got home, and the chance to commit lots of sins which could be forgiven on arrival at the shrine. The Wife of Bath clearly enjoys her pilgrimages in this way: her three visits to Jerusalem, and her trips to Rome, to Santiago da Compostela and to Cologne argue either a sanctity of which there is not the least sign in her portrait or her prologue, or the readiness to spend lots of money on something that was extremely pleasurable to her. Chaucer's delicious remark, 'She coude muchel of wandrynge by the weye' (l.467) clearly means more than one sort of exploration.

In the first place, then, the pilgrimage frame allows Chaucer not only to be inclusive in a *tour de force* of literary dexterity; it allows him also to raise throughout the book important questions about the truth and value of fiction. The Parson, himself fictional, is made in his prologue to reject fiction and refuse all value to story: only a sermon can be of any use to sinful men. And, final irony, the whole collection is a *story* retold from his avowedly faulty memory by one of the fictional pilgrims, 'Chaucer'.

Further, the pilgrimage-frame allows Chaucer to focus the

discussion of really important issues sharply on the world in which he and his audience moved daily. The Tabard, and an innkeeper called Harry Bailly, actually existed. The campaigns the Knight had just returned from were real ones, on which many of Chaucer's contemporaries had actually served. Some of the pilgrims have an oblique — 'now you see it, now you don't' — resemblance to real historical individuals (like Harry Bailly, indeed) in Chaucer's own day, yet cannot be identified with them. The poem cannot be mere journalism: it is impossible for Chaucer to be describing what he really saw, for he tells us things only an omniscient poet could have known — not only the inner thoughts and attitudes of many of his figures, but also what *nobody* knew. Of the Merchant, for example, he says 'Ther wiste no wight that he was in dette' (1.280); the Sergeant's impressive busy-ness is slyly under cut by 'yet he semed bisier than he was' (1.322). Chaucer is anchoring his fiction in the real world so that the lens of fiction can be used, often uncomfortably, to evaluate and analyse it. Fiction, especially romances, however serious and profound they might be, had up to this time often been set either in a nebulous past or in a locale reduced to virtual nonentity in order to focus on the ethical and moral issues. But here Chaucer is tu ning the real world of late fourteenth century England, where real people went on real pilgrimages starting from Southwark, into his symbolic locale.

Finally, without exception the pilgrimage in medieval literature (and in life!) is seen as analogous to the Way, the life of man on earth on his journey to Judgement and — one hopes — the heavenly Jerusalem. The life of all men — Chaucer's readers then and now included — is in some sense a pilgrimage. The point is emphasised when Chaucer makes the Parson, who tells the tale immediately preceding the arrival of the pilgrims at Canterbury, point the parallel, drawing on Jesus's words, 'I am the Way, the Truth and the Life':

> And Jhesu, for his grace, wit me sende
> To shewe yow the wey, in this viage,
> Of thilke parfit glorious pilgrymage
> That highte Jerusalem celestial

(X, ll.48–51)

The pilgrimage motif therefore provides not only a metaphor

that focuses the entire story about the telling of tales with a seriousness that is disconcerting; it is also an elegant inclusive frame that evaluates the figures who appear in it, laughing and 'pleying' as they travel towards a judgement few of them take seriously but which is the inevitable end of their journey and which none of them can escape.

1

The frame-story, therefore, is crucial to the design of the poem. But that frame-story cannot just start; it has to be properly prepared for if we are to read it with the subtlety and attention Chaucer wanted. The job of preparation falls, naturally enough, to the *Prologue*. Nothing could be further from the truth than to see it as merely an introduction to be got over as quickly as possible in order to get to the tales, or as a simple catalogue written merely for the sake of describing characters in a more or less vivid way. It has to engage the audience's interest from the very first line; it has to introduce some of the major themes that the whole work will explore, and establish the figures (and the values Chaucer wishes to attach to them) who will later become characters in the continuing story told in the headlinks, and the tellers of the tales; it has also to establish the narratorial voice of the comic distortion of himself Chaucer wrote into the poem. (Let us call Chaucer-in-the-poem the *persona* — the Latin word means 'mask'.)

The ideas in the *Prologue*'s opening lines are so important that discussion of them is best left to the end of this essay. The narrative really begins with the suggestive word 'Bifil' (l.19) — 'It happened', or 'it chanced'. Chance and coincidence, or their antitheses, order and purpose, are major themes in the whole collection. That word 'Bifil' underlines that although individual characters may have, like 'Chaucer', gone to the Tabard Inn on purpose to start the pilgrimage, the actual group is thrown together by chance. References to chance abound in the *Prologue*: in line 844, for example, Chaucer stresses that what may seem like chance may not be chance at all, for the Knight draws the short straw in the drawing of lots:

> Were it by aventure, or sort, or cas

As the man of highest rank in the company, he could naturally have taken precedence in the telling of tales. He submits to the Host's game, yet chance confirms the ordered hierarchy to which he belongs and which he represents.

Moreover, because it is a pilgrimage that is in question, the *Prologue* cannot be separated entirely from the links between the tales. For a pilgrimage, symbolic or real, necessarily involves movement through space and time. Now the most natural metaphor of all for the life of man is the passing of a day from sunrise to sunset. In the headlinks to the tales, where we are back in the narrative level of the road to Canterbury, Chaucer often makes us aware of time passing. The idea of the night coming, when no man may work, hangs over the whole poem, giving its moral exploration an urgency that perhaps only the Pardoner, in his twisted way, and the Parson appreciate. Spatially, too, the cavalcade is insecure: it is displaced from towns, always between them, or just approaching them, or outside them altogether. It is suggestive that of the places Chaucer mentions, Southwark even two centuries later was a place of low amusement and lower reputation; that the Watering Place of St Thomas was a place of execution for the county of Surrey; and that towns, representative of civilised values — the heavenly Jerusalem is after all a city — are seen only in the distance. The outskirts and suburbs were sinister and disreputable places in history as well as fiction. In *The Canterbury Tales* the rogue alchemist Canon lives in the suburbs; the Miller with his bagpipe (symbolic of disorder and lecherousness, as the paintings of Hieronymus Bosch and Brueghel remind us) leads the cavalcade out of town (*Prologue*, — 1.566); the old man in *The Pardoner's Tale* is going towards (but has not yet reached) a village, seeking death, and sends the rioters on a crooked way — off the beaten track — to find ... death. There are many other examples; the point is that the frame-story, and therefore the *Prologue*, is an epitome of society cast adrift into a moral and spiritual wilderness, hoping eventually to find salvation in an Abiding City (*Parson's Tale* — X, ll.12, 19, 30ff, 46ff, 63,

70f). And among the little flock are the predators, masquerading as what they are not — the Pardoner and the Canon. This important symbol, superimposed on a glimpse of a real, believable England, must affect our final view of the whole work.

The apparent randomness of the assembly of these pilgrims masks another valuing device. There are only four whose excellence is fully endorsed both by the *persona*, and by the objective judgement of an audience: the Knight, the Plowman, the Clerk and the Parson. The usual medieval understanding of society was to see it as divided into three mutually interdependent Estates: those who work (e.g. the Plowman), those who fight (e.g. the Knight), and those who pray (e.g. the 'active' Parson and the 'contemplative' Clerk[1]).

The ideal worker worked selflessly for the community, and while he did so was protected and defended by the selfless valour of the ideal fighting man. His spiritual needs were looked after by the ideal religious, who tirelessly visited the sick and ministered to his flock, or indefatigably sought wisdom and understanding in study. Chaucer is therefore providing us, in those characters who fulfil the proper obligations of their role, with moral yardsticks by which to judge all the others who must, by definition, fit into one of the Three Estates. And when the *persona* sympathises with, or approves of, characters who betray those ideals — as in the case of the Monk, or Prioress — we can be sure that we are getting a warning that something is very badly wrong indeed, not only with what that character represents but also with the way society, represented by the naïve narrator, tolerates them.

The *Prologue*, then, is no mere gallery of vivid characters — or caricatures — but a serious moral analysis of an entire society that, often uncaring and unaware, is under imminent judgement. It could well be argued that the *Tales* as a whole take that analysis further, and that just as no character can be understood without references to the principles, expectations and values underlying the notion of the Three Estates and

---

[1] The familiar distinction between the *Vita Activa* and the *Vita Contemplativa*, given authority in the Gospels by the distinctions between Martha and Mary (Luke 10).

exemplified in the ideal characters, so too, in the end, no tale can be understood without reference to all the others.

2

The descriptions of the pilgrims are very odd — odd not only in the way the pilgrims are deliberately grouped in no sort of order when order and rank were fundamental to the way men thought about society and the universe itself, but also in the lack of structure in each description. The medieval arts of rhetoric laid down fairly rigid guidelines for describing people: if one wanted to describe appearance, for example, the description regularly had a settled pattern, starting at the top of the head and systematically working down to the feet, employing appropriate metaphor and simile meanwhile to create a brightly lit, sharply visualised picture like those in the miniatures in manuscripts. Or, alternatively, one could choose to describe moral qualities: again, there was a regular pattern and list of headings designed to do this effectively and efficiently. These techniques of *effictio* and *descriptio* were perfectly well known to Chaucer and expected by his audience. Yet in the *Prologue* he plays ducks and drakes with them: internal and external qualities, normally kept separate, are randomly mixed; no character gets a detailed and complete description, Chaucer choosing rather to give us a hotchpotch of characteristics, features, blemishes, mannerisms and thoughts of wildly divergent importance. Since Chaucer knew perfectly well how to handle the techniques of description, and can do so elsewhere, this jumbling and its inevitable effect of shock, unease and puzzlement on its first audience must clearly be intentional, a device which forces attention on a theme which runs throughout the book — that of making us think again about what we thought we knew.

The most important immediate effect, though, is the characterisation of the narrator, whether the poem was read aloud to an audience or read as a text by an individual reader. In a sentence of notable clumsiness (ll.35–41), Chaucer stresses that what we are getting is the *persona's* memory of how they '*semed*' to him — his impressions, no more: that is, we are already two removes from whatever reality these figures might have had. Moreover, Chaucer later underlines the general lack of order by making the *persona* stress that he has 'nat set folk in hir degree/. . . as that they sholde stonde' (1.744–745) because '[His] wit is short' (1.746). Yet in the same passage he vigorously asserts that he is bound by 'truth', and has to relate things exactly as they were in appropriate language (ll.730ff). Clearly, the issues that are being raised are complex. The *persona*, the poet disguised, misremembers; bound to be a truth-teller, all he can be true to is his own perception, not an objective reality. Knowing, too, how things ought to be done, he has not so done them. What, then, are we to make of his judgements when he gives us them? What are we to infer of what he has *not* said? A reader or an audience can hardly help accepting *a priori* a narrator as a trustworthy guide, yet the effect of this narration is to make this one utterly untrustworthy, and to force us to use our own judgement — and to think about the way we arrive at it, in reality or in reading.

That Chaucer's strategic aim is in large part the establishment of the *persona* as a sort of moral idiot, not to be trusted yet all too easy for the incautious to accept, is supported by the way he introduces himself. The real Chaucer was acknowledged as the supreme poet of his age, and he was fully aware of and partly sympathised with the high claims made by the Italian theorists like Dante, Boccaccio and Petrarch for the poet and his status as a channel for the Wisdom of God Himself. His first audience knew very well that he was no incompetent nincompoop. But at the very beginning, he presents himself as about to start his pilgrimage — that is, as also a man under judgement as are all the rest in that metaphorical journey. When he introduces himself directly into the narrative again, at lines 542–544, he groups himself in the last place one would expect — with the Reeve, the Summoner, the Pardoner, and the Manciple — a rag, tag and bobtail of rogues and cheats who abuse their positions of trust and authority. The poet has a position of trust and authority too: as Chaucer underlines elsewhere, he constitutes the memory of a society, passing on the wisdom of the past to the present and future. The coolly inconsequential association of the *persona* with this group of villains must not only underline his specific unreliability as a guide in

E

this poem, but must demand too that expectations of what poets and poetry do be examined and their validity tested. When in the tales themselves we find questions of the status and value of poetry, of ambiguity of knowledge, judgement and understanding constantly being raised, and find too that 'Chaucer' tells two tales of signal incompetence, it is hard not to conclude that this treatment of the *persona* in the *Prologue* is designed to open up a major theme in the whole collection. For many tales turn on characters in them construing reality in ways which they want to believe in, seeing a world not as it in fact is but as they want it to be or as their muddled vision or thought allows them to see it.

This same subjectivity of judgement underlies the *persona's* narrative in the *Prologue*. Consider, for example, the use of value words. Take 'worthy' and 'gentil': words that quite properly and quite without any irony are applied to the Knight (ll.43, 72). The portrait is after all of the ideal fighting man: this rather austere and forbidding figure fights only to defend Christendom, not, like his lightweight and frivolous son the Squire, using arms merely to raid fellow-Christians 'In hope to stonden in his lady grace' (l.88). (That we find the Squire much more attractive is meant to tell us something about ourselves.) But what are we to think of the judgement of someone who uses the words correctly, as here, and then applies them to obvious rogues like the Friar (ll.243, 269), Summoner (l.647) and Pardoner (l.669), and other ambivalent figures like Merchant (l.279), Franklin (l.360), and Manciple (567)? The effect of the repeated word is at once to reduce the integrity of the narrator's judgement and to remind us of what these words really ought to mean — thus, in fact, judging these characters very harshly indeed. We hear the bland voice of the *persona*, but these apparently anodyne words in it force us to judge both the character and his describer.

Similarly, the selection of details shows the same irony: a type of irony which is developed more extensively in the tales, as when the Wife of Bath, the Pardoner, or the Franklin, for example, are unaware of the implications both in general and specifically for themselves of the stories they tell. The description of the Prioress tells us little or nothing about her life as a religious — one must presume she had one; the selection of details reveals that the *persona* responded to her as a beautiful woman and potential sex object. His acceptance of her self-indulgent sentimentality as charity (ll.143ff) reveals that his judgement is completely foxed by her femininity. Describing her (or not), he is describing himself. Similarly, the Monk: this man breaks every rule in the book and roundly rejects the book itself (ll.177ff); having theoretically forsaken the world to concentrate on the things of God, he is more worldly — and more successful — than most who have made no such profession. Yet the tone is one of admiration, almost of envy in the enumeration of his possessions: the overpowering personality of the Monk, his social attractiveness and clout has so bamboozled the timid *persona* that:

> . . . I seyde his opinion was good.
>
> (l.183)

And as there were all too many worldly religious about like the Monk and the Prioress, the *persona*'s acceptance of them mirrors in little the disturbing fuzziness of standards in a society that tolerates such gross dereliction of sacred duties, of literally life and death importance.

All these portraits have roots in the society of Chaucer's day, in its values, its current affairs, its in-jokes, its snobbisms, and its abuses and failings. But the real brilliance lies in their being imagined *as they would have been remembered* by a man of limited intelligence, social ineptness and moral confusion. Thus, in an important anticipation of the stance we are often asked to adopt to the narrative of the pilgrimage and to the tales both individually and as groups, we are able to stand towards the *persona* much as Providence might stand towards us: even though we only see what he tells us, we see more than he does, for we are seeing him telling it and judging (as he is not) his selection of details.

The discrete, timeless and virtually soundless portraits of the pilgrims once assembled, the *Prologue* suddenly bursts into life and sound and movement. It is as if the characters have been brought mute one by one onto the stage, have been introduced, and now they can be put to use. They begin to interact, and their interaction is always significant. For example, the

Host elects himself master of this pilgrimage (a sort of Master of the Caravan).[2]

By rank this job ought to have fallen to the Knight, and it is not fanciful to see the Host as a sort of Lord of Misrule whose authority was absolute for the short period convention allowed it to last. It is he who (cannily) proposes the contest — of which we too must be judges — and it is he who devises the choosing of the first teller by lot — by chance. Ironically, Chance confirms the hierarchy that has just been denied: the Knight begins the tale-telling, just as the Knight's was quite properly the first description. The interest in Chance and Order which we see in *The Knight's Tale* and *The Miller's Tale* is present also in the frame-story: here, the noble Knight accepts the order imposed by the Host, while later the ignoble and disordered Miller reduces even this temporary order to chaotic quarrelling and personal abuse. What has happened in the *Prologue* and the frame-story is an exact analogy, a model, of the sort of reading Chaucer wants us to give to the individual tales. For each, like the individual silent portraits, must at first be seen on its own, floating detached from all others in the world it itself creates. Then it can — to a greater or lesser degree — be attached to its narrator, giving it a further level of meaning and significance. Then, finally, it is brought into the whole dynamic and symbolic discussion of *The Canterbury Tales*, where each tale is no longer on its own but part of another story. And finally, the *Prologue* provides us with a set of standards for our reading of the tales. For just as the Knight values all the other fighting men in the *Prologue*, he provides a standard for all knights in the tales, as the Clerk does for students, the Parson for priests and religious, and the Plowman for artisans and tradesmen. An obscenely distorted image of the Clerk of Oxford appears in Nicholas in *The Miller's Tale*, or in Alan and John in the Reeve's; and we glimpse Alison of Bath in the Miller's Alison of Oxford. The setting of things side by side without open comment is one of Chaucer's techniques for making us think and judge in the

---

[2] The problem of safety while travelling meant that people would wait in the inns until a largish group had assembled, and then set out in company under a leader who knew the way — like the caravans of the Near East.

Prologue; it is extended into the way he balances tales, plots and characters in the body of the book.

3

What, then, of the opening lines? Opening a poem in April, when the sun is in Aries, the constellation of the Creation of the World and the first morning in Eden, makes some emphatic signals to an audience. They could hardly not expect a poem on Love, for such poems almost invariably started in springtime with a description of the beauty of the fresh green landscape and the 'wild music' of the birds mirroring the harmony of the heavens. And love is one of the enduring human interests, which even today shows no sign of going out of fashion. Yet here too, apparently, Chaucer leads his audience up the garden path, for there seems to be no mention of love at all.

The teasing is serious enough: it is designed to make us think. The first hint of something odd is the line that follows 'So priketh hem nature in hir corages' (l.11), with its sexual play on words: the birds' sexual desires are seen as of a piece with the restlessness that drives men to seek far shrines and shores, and go on pilgrimage to seek healing. We must, I think, realise that Chaucer is using what could be the opening of a standard sort of poem of love between man and woman to signal that he is talking about a much more important type of love: the love that is the mainspring of the universe.

In *Troilus and Criseyde* Book III, lines 1–49, Chaucer stresses — by no means unconventionally — that the principle of love extends in the universe from the force that keeps the planets singing on their courses right down to order in societies, in homes and families, to the love of man for woman and the desire of beast and bird for their mates. Love is thus an emotional, social, political, physical and cosmic force, deriving ultimately from the God Who is Love. The sexual desire that motivates Nicholas and Alison in *The Miller's Tale* is — however distantly — related to the Love that created the Universe. When Chaucer's friend, John Gower, came to write his long *Confessio Amantis* at about the same time as *The*

Canterbury Tales, he explored first in his Prologue the ramifi-
cations of this cosmic love. He then moved logically on to the
discussion of love, or lack of it in proper form, in the individual:
the individual is, in his complex of balanced or contradictory
elements and emotions, an image of society and thus of the
cosmos. So the body of the poem, where a lover discusses his
failures in love with a confessor, consists of a great number
of stories told by the confessor in illustration of his moral
advice, exploring the way men and women behave. It is most
attractive to see *The Canterbury Tales* in a similar way. The
stories — and many of them turn on types of love, or the misuse
or misunderstanding of love — offer a vast range of insights into
the potentialities of human behaviour. The inclusiveness that
we saw above as so striking a feature of Chaucer's design thus
allows him to range right across the subject. But those stories
are set in a little community which quarrels, disagrees, has
problems with order and knowledge and judgement, that is an
image of society in general; and this little community is moving
through space and time on its way to Judgment and, one hopes,
healing, where each shall know as they are known. The opening
story, the Knight's, is one which asserts that behind all the
apparent disorder and suffering of the universe is an ordered
and loving Providence; the one that closes the collection is a
sermon that analyses what is wrong with man, and offers hope
of reform and forgiveness. Between those two the other stories
run the whole gamut of human types, human love, human
suffering. Thus the connection in the opening lines of pilgrimage
and the seeking of healing with love is fully justified; and the
surprise we feel when it is first made alerts us to a major theme
of the whole book.

The *Prologue*, then, is essential to a properly focused
reading of the book. It provides standards to guide us through
a maze deliberately perplexing, for the truth is never simple; in
establishing the figure of the *persona* it alerts us to the questions that are to be discussed of the nature and status of fiction
and the poet's art, the necessity and yet the impossibility of
judgement; it opens up the major themes of order, truth, justice
and love that are explored, even in an incomplete poem, with
inexhaustible subtlety and resource.

AFTERTHOUGHTS

1

What use, according to Moseley, does Chaucer make of the pilgrimage frame?

2

Explain the significance of the 'Three Estates' (page 111) to Moseley's reading of the *General Prologue*.

3

What do you understand by '*a priori*' (page 113)?

4

Compare Moseley's commentary on the Knight (page 114) with that of Norgate (pages 11–14) and Oliver (pages 83–86).

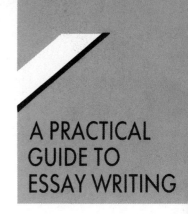

A PRACTICAL GUIDE TO ESSAY WRITING

INTRODUCTION

First, a word of warning. Good essays are the product of a creative engagement with literature. So never try to restrict your studies to what you think will be 'useful in the exam'. Ironically, you will restrict your grade potential if you do.

This doesn't mean, of course, that you should ignore the basic skills of essay writing. When you read critics, make a conscious effort to notice *how* they communicate their ideas. The guidelines that follow offer advice of a more explicit kind. But they are no substitute for practical experience. It is never easy to express ideas with clarity and precision. But the more often you tackle the problems involved and experiment to find your own voice, the more fluent you will become. So practise writing essays as often as possible.

HOW TO PLAN
AN ESSAY

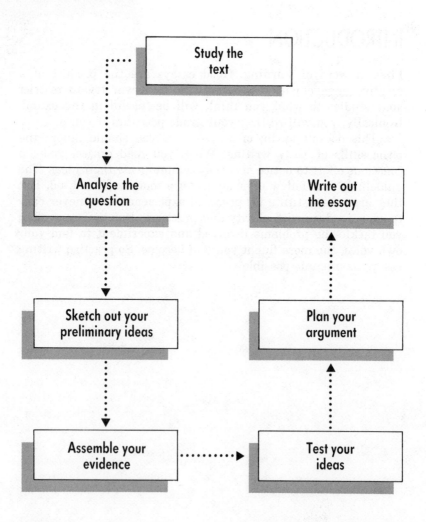

Study the
text

Analyse the
question

Write out
the essay

Sketch out your
preliminary ideas

Plan your
argument

Assemble your
evidence

Test your
ideas

Study the text

The first step in writing a good essay is to get to know the set text well. Never write about a text until you are fully familiar with it. Even a discussion of the opening chapter of a novel, for example, should be informed by an understanding of the book as a whole. Literary texts, however, are by their very nature complex and on a first reading you are bound to miss many significant features. Re-read the book with care, if possible more than once. Look up any unfamiliar words in a good dictionary and if the text you are studying was written more than a few decades ago, consult the *Oxford English Dictionary* to find out whether the meanings of any terms have shifted in the intervening period.

Good books are difficult to put down when you first read them. But a more leisurely second or third reading gives you the opportunity to make notes on those features you find significant. An index of characters and events is often useful, particularly when studying novels with a complex plot or time scheme. The main aim, however, should be to record your *responses* to the text. By all means note, for example, striking images. But be sure to add *why* you think them striking. Similarly, record any thoughts you may have on interesting comparisons with other texts, puzzling points of characterisation, even what you take to be aesthetic blemishes. The important thing is to annotate fully and adventurously. The most seemingly idiosyncratic comment may later lead to a crucial area of discussion which you would otherwise have overlooked. It helps to have a working copy of the text in which to mark up key passages and jot down marginal comments (although obviously these practices are taboo when working with library, borrowed or valuable copies!). But keep a fuller set of notes as well and organise these under appropriate headings.

Literature does not exist in an aesthetic vacuum, however, and you should try to find out as much as possible about the context of its production and reception. It is particularly important to read other works by the same author and writings by contemporaries. At this early stage, you may want to restrict your secondary reading to those standard reference works, such as biographies, which are widely available in public libraries. In the long run, however, it pays to read as wide a range of critical studies as possible.

Some students, and tutors, worry that such studies may stifle the development of any truly personal response. But this won't happen if you are alert to the danger and read critically. After all, you wouldn't passively accept what a stranger told you in conversation. The fact that a critic's views are in print does not necessarily make them any more authoritative (as a glance at the review pages of the *TLS* and *London Review of Books* will reveal). So question the views you find: 'Does this critic's interpretation agree with mine and where do we part company?' 'Can it be right to try and restrict this text's meanings to those found by its author or first audience?' 'Doesn't this passage treat a theatrical text as though it were a novel?' Often it is views which you reject which prove most valuable since they challenge you to articulate your own position with greater clarity. Be sure to keep careful notes on what the critic wrote, and your *reactions* to what the critic wrote.

Analyse the question

You cannot begin to answer a question until you understand what task it is you have been asked to perform. Re-cast the question in your own words and reconstruct the line of reasoning which lies behind it. Where there is a choice of topics, try to choose the one for which you are best prepared. It would, for example, be unwise to tackle 'How far do you agree that in *Paradise Lost* Milton transformed the epic models he inherited from ancient Greece and Rome?' without a working knowledge of Homer and Virgil (or *Paradise Lost* for that matter!). If you do not already know the works of these authors, the question should spur you on to read more widely — or discourage you from attempting it at all. The scope of an essay, however, is not always so obvious and you must remain alert to the implied demands of each question. How could you possibly 'Consider the view that *Wuthering Heights* transcends the conventions of the Gothic novel' without reference to at least some of those works which, the question suggests, have *not* transcended Gothic conventions?

When you have decided on a topic, analyse the terms of the question itself. Sometimes these self-evidently require careful definition: *tragedy* and *irony*, for example, are notoriously difficult concepts to pin down and you will probably need to consult a good dictionary of literary terms. Don't ignore, however, those seemingly innocuous phrases which often smuggle in significant assumptions. 'Does Macbeth lack the nobility of the true tragic hero?' obviously invites you to discuss nobility and the nature of the tragic hero. But what of 'lack' and 'true' — do they suggest that the play would be improved had Shakespeare depicted Macbeth in a different manner? or that tragedy is superior to other forms of drama? Remember that you are not expected meekly to agree with the assumptions implicit in the question. Some questions are deliberately provocative in order to stimulate an engaged response. Don't be afraid to take up the challenge.

Sketch out your preliminary ideas

'Which comes first, the evidence or the answer?' is one of those chicken and egg questions. How can you form a view without inspecting the evidence? But how can you know which evidence is relevant without some idea of what it is you are looking for? In practice the mind reviews evidence and formulates preliminary theories or hypotheses at one and the same time, although for the sake of clarity we have separated out the processes. Remember that these early ideas are only there to get you started. You *expect* to modify them in the light of the evidence you uncover. Your initial hypothesis may be an instinctive 'gut-reaction'. Or you may find that you prefer to 'sleep on the problem', allowing ideas to gell over a period of time. Don't worry in either case. The mind is quite capable of processing a vast amount of accumulated evidence, the product of previous reading and thought, and reaching sophisticated intuitive judgements. Eventually, however, you are going to have to think carefully through any ideas you arrive at by such intuitive processes. Are they logical? Do they take account of all the relevant factors? Do they fully answer the question set? Are there any obvious reasons to qualify or abandon them?

Assemble your evidence

Now is the time to return to the text and re-read it with the question and your working hypothesis firmly in mind. Many of the notes you have already made are likely to be useful, but assess the precise relevance of this material and make notes on any new evidence you discover. The important thing is to cast your net widely and take into account points which tend to undermine your case as well as those that support it. As always, ensure that your notes are full, accurate, and reflect your own critical judgements.

You may well need to go outside the text if you are to do full justice to the question. If you think that the 'Oedipus complex' may be relevant to an answer on *Hamlet* then read Freud and a balanced selection of those critics who have discussed the appropriateness of applying psychoanalytical theories to the interpretation of literature. Their views can most easily be tracked down by consulting the annotated bibliographies held by most major libraries (and don't be afraid to ask a librarian for help in finding and using these). Remember that you go to works of criticism not only to obtain information but to stimulate you into clarifying your own position. And that since life is short and many critical studies are long, judicious use of a book's index and/or contents list is not to be scorned. You can save yourself a great deal of future labour if you carefully record full bibliographic details at this stage.

Once you have collected the evidence, organise it coherently. Sort the detailed points into related groups and identify the quotations which support these. You must also assess the relative importance of each point, for in an essay of limited length it is essential to establish a firm set of priorities, exploring some ideas in depth while discarding or subordinating others.

Test your ideas

As we stressed earlier, a hypothesis is only a proposal, and one that you fully expect to modify. Review it with the evidence before you. Do you really still believe in it? It would be surprising if you did not want to modify it in some way. If you cannot see any problems, others may. Try discussing your ideas with friends and relatives. Raise them in class discussions. Your tutor is certain to welcome your initiative. The critical process is essentially collaborative and there is absolutely no reason why you should not listen to and benefit from the views of others. Similarly, you should feel free to test your ideas against the theories put forward in academic journals and books. But do not just borrow what you find. Critically analyse the views on offer and, where appropriate, integrate them into your own pattern of thought. You must, of course, give full acknowledgement to the sources of such views.

Do not despair if you find you have to abandon or modify significantly your initial position. The fact that you are prepared to do so is a mark of intellectual integrity. Dogmatism is never an academic virtue and many of the best essays explore the *process* of scholarly enquiry rather than simply record its results.

Plan your argument

Once you have more or less decided on your attitude to the question (for an answer is never really 'finalised') you have to present your case in the most persuasive manner. In order to do this you must avoid meandering from point to point and instead produce an organised argument — a structured flow of ideas and supporting evidence, leading logically to a conclusion which fully answers the question. Never begin to write until you have produced an outline of your argument.

You may find it easiest to begin by sketching out its main stage as a flow chart or some other form of visual presentation. But eventually you should produce a list of paragraph topics. The paragraph is the conventional written demarcation for a unit of thought and you can outline an argument quite simply by briefly summarising the substance of each paragraph and then checking that these points (you may remember your English teacher referring to them as topic sentences) really do follow a coherent order. Later you will be able to elaborate on each topic, illustrating and qualifying it as you go along. But you will find this far easier to do if you possess from the outset a clear map of where you are heading.

All questions require some form of an argument. Even so-called 'descriptive' questions *imply* the need for an argument. An adequate answer to the request to 'Outline the role of Iago in *Othello*' would do far more than simply list his appearances on stage. It would at the very least attempt to provide some *explanation* for his actions — is he, for example, a representative stage 'Machiavel'? an example of pure evil, 'motiveless malignity'? or a realistic study of a tormented personality reacting to identifiable social and psychological pressures?

Your conclusion ought to address the terms of the question. It may seem obvious, but 'how far do you agree', 'evaluate', 'consider', 'discuss', etc, are *not* interchangeable formulas and your conclusion must take account of the precise wording of the question. If asked 'How far do you agree?', the concluding paragraph of your essay really should state whether you are in complete agreement, total disagreement, or, more likely, partial agreement. Each preceding paragraph should have a clear justification for its existence and help to clarify the reasoning which underlies your conclusion. If you find that a paragraph serves no good purpose (perhaps merely summarising the plot), • do not hesitate to discard it.

The arrangement of the paragraphs, the overall strategy of the argument, can vary. One possible pattern is dialectical: present the arguments in favour of one point of view (**thesis**); then turn to counter-arguments or to a rival interpretation (**antithesis**); finally evaluate the competing claims and arrive at your own conclusion (**synthesis**). You may, on the other hand, feel so convinced of the merits of one particular case that you wish to devote your entire essay to arguing that viewpoint persuasively (although it is always desirable to indicate, however briefly, that you are aware of alternative, if flawed, positions). As the essays contained in this volume demonstrate, there are many other possible strategies. Try to adopt the one which will most comfortably accommodate the demands of the question and allow you to express your thoughts with the greatest possible clarity.

Be careful, however, not to apply abstract formulas in a mechanical manner. It is true that you should be careful to define your terms. It is *not* true that every essay should begin with 'The dictionary defines *x* as . . .'. In fact, definitions are often best left until an appropriate moment for their introduction arrives. Similarly every essay should have a beginning, middle and end. But it does not follow that in your opening paragraph you should announce an intention to write an essay, or that in your concluding paragraph you need to signal an imminent desire to put down your pen. The old adages are often useful reminders of what constitutes good practice, but they must be interpreted intelligently.

Write out the essay

Once you have developed a coherent argument you should aim to communicate it in the most effective manner possible. Make certain you clearly identify yourself, and the question you are answering. Ideally, type your answer, or at least ensure your handwriting is legible and that you leave sufficient space for your tutor's comments. Careless presentation merely distracts from the force of your argument. Errors of grammar, syntax and spelling are far more serious. At best they are an irritating blemish, particularly in the work of a student who should be sensitive to the nuances of language. At worst, they seriously confuse the sense of your argument. If you are aware that you have stylistic problems of this kind, ask your tutor for advice at the earliest opportunity. Everyone, however, is liable to commit the occasional howler. The only remedy is to give yourself plenty of time in which to proof-read your manuscript (often reading it aloud is helpful) before submitting it.

Language, however, is not only an instrument of communication; it is also an instrument of thought. If you want to think clearly and precisely you should strive for a clear, precise prose style. Keep your sentences short and direct. Use modern, straightforward English wherever possible. Avoid repetition, clichés and wordiness. Beware of generalisations, simplifications, and overstatements. Orwell analysed the relationship between stylistic vice and muddled thought in his essay 'Politics and the English Language' (1946) — it remains essential reading (and is still readily available in volume 4 of the Penguin *Collected Essays, Journalism and Letters*). Generalisations, for example, are always dangerous. They are rarely true and tend to suppress the individuality of the texts in question. A remark such as 'Keats always employs sensuous language in his poetry' is not only fatuous (what, after all, does it mean? is *every* word he wrote equally 'sensuous'?) but tends to obscure interesting distinctions which could otherwise be made between, say, the descriptions in the 'Ode on a Grecian Urn' and those in 'To Autumn'.

The intelligent use of quotations can help you make your points with greater clarity. Don't sprinkle them throughout your essay without good reason. There is no need, for example, to use them to support uncontentious statements of fact. 'Macbeth murdered Duncan' does not require textual evidence (unless you wish to dispute Thurber's brilliant parody, 'The Macbeth Murder Mystery', which reveals Lady Macbeth's father as the culprit!). Quotations should be included, however, when they are necessary to support your case. The proposition that Macbeth's imaginative powers wither after he has killed his king would certainly require extensive quotation: you would almost certainly want to analyse key passages from both before and after the murder (perhaps his first and last soliloquies?). The key word here is 'analyse'. Quotations cannot make your points on their own. It is up to you to demonstrate their relevance and clearly explain to your readers *why* you want them to focus on the passage you have selected.

Most of the academic conventions which govern the presentation of essays are set out briefly in the style sheet below. The question of gender, however, requires fuller discussion. More than half the population of the world is female. Yet many writers still refer to an undifferentiated *man*kind. Or write of the author and *his* public. We do not think that this convention has much to recommend it. At the very least, it runs the risk of introducing unintended sexist attitudes. And at times leads to such patent absurdities as 'Cleopatra's final speech asserts *man*'s true nobility'. With a little thought, you can normally find ways of expressing yourself which do not suggest that the typical author, critic or reader is male. Often you can simply use plural forms, which is probably a more elegant solution than relying on such awkward formulations as 's/he' or 'he and she'. You should also try to avoid distinguishing between male and female authors on the basis of forenames. Why *Jane* Austen and not *George* Byron? Refer to all authors by their last names unless there is some good reason not to. Where there may otherwise be confusion, say between T S and George Eliot, give the name in full when it first occurs and thereafter use the last name only.

Finally, keep your audience firmly in mind. Tutors and examiners are interested in understanding your conclusions and the processes by which you arrived at them. They are not interested in reading a potted version of a book they already know. **So don't pad out your work with plot summary.**

Hints for examinations

In an examination you should go through exactly the same processes as you would for the preparation of a term essay. The only difference lies in the fact that some of the stages will have had to take place before you enter the examination room. This should not bother you unduly. Examiners are bound to avoid the merely eccentric when they come to formulate papers and if you have read widely and thought deeply about the central issues raised by your set texts you can be confident you will have sufficient material to answer the majority of questions sensibly.

The fact that examinations impose strict time limits makes it *more* rather than less, important that you plan carefully. There really is no point in floundering into an answer without any idea of where you are going, particularly when there will not be time to recover from the initial error.

Before you begin to answer any question at all, study the entire paper with care. Check that you understand the rubric and know how many questions you have to answer and whether any are compulsory. It may be comforting to spot a title you feel confident of answering well, but don't rush to tackle it: read *all* the questions before deciding which *combination* will allow you to display your abilities to the fullest advantage. Once you have made your choice, analyse each question, sketch out your ideas, assemble the evidence, review your initial hypothesis, plan your argument, *before* trying to write out an answer. And make notes at each stage: not only will these help you arrive at a sensible conclusion, but examiners are impressed by evidence of careful thought.

Plan your time as well as your answers. If you have practised writing timed essays as part of your revision, you should not find this too difficult. There can be a temptation to allocate extra time to the questions you know you can answer well; but this is always a short-sighted policy. You will find yourself left to face a question which would in any event have given you difficulty without even the time to give it serious thought. It is, moreover, easier to gain marks at the lower end of the scale than at the upper, and you will never compensate for one poor answer by further polishing two satisfactory answers. Try to leave some time at the end of the examination to re-read your answers and correct any obvious errors. If the worst comes to the worst and you run short of time, don't just keep writing until you are forced to break off in mid-paragraph. It is far better to provide for the examiner a set of notes which indicate the overall direction of your argument.

Good luck — but if you prepare for the examination conscientiously and tackle the paper in a methodical manner, you won't need it!

Longer verse quotation indented and introduced by a colon. Quotation marks are not needed. The line reference is given directly after the quotation, in brackets.

estate. The Monk's outlay would cover the employment of similar tough men, totally proficient:

> (Wel koude he dresse his takel yemanly;
> His arwes drouped noght with fetheres lowe)
>
> (ll.106–107)

and additionally armed with 'a swerd and a bokeler' (l.112), and a murderously sharp 'gay daggere' (l.113). The Monk can afford to make as much noise as he likes with his jingling bridle; the preservation of his hunting is in the hands of those who melt into the background, perhaps 'in cote and hood of grene' (l.103). Hunting and the preservation of game in the late fourteenth century is a political act to be seen in relation to a volatile society which did indeed boil over in the Rising of 1381. Rosamond Faith explains:

Long prose quotation indented and introduced by a colon. Quotation marks are not needed.

Three dots (ellipsis) indicate where words or phrases have been cut from a quotation.

> Although poaching obviously has an economic aspect, it seems to have had in the middle ages, as later, a vital though largely unspoken ideological aspect as well. The idea that the peasantry were entitled to what the land naturally provided conflicted with the seigneurial notion that lordship implied *dominium* over all the assets of the manor.... Poaching, primarily of deer, was a political issue in the late fourteenth century, and was seen as such by contemporaries. The Patent Rolls of the 1360s to 1380s are crowded with reports... of large-scale poaching raids on the property of the gentry, the aristocracy and the royal family, in which taking deer was combined with attacking manor houses, claiming common rights and burning manorial rolls.[1]

indication of footnote

The ostentatious self-confidence of the Monk who parades the trappings of wealth, the sleeves 'purfiled at the hond/ With grys' (ll.193–194), and his boast that:

> Ful many a deyntee hors hadde he in stable

constitute a challenge to anyone unwilling to acc prevailing social structure. Society is not background; shaping force.

Short verse quotation incorporated into the text of the essay within quotation marks. Line endings are indicated by a slash (/).

---

[1] Rosamond Faith, 'The "Great Rumour" of 1377 and Peasant Ideology', in R H Hilton and T H Aston (eds), *The English Rising of 1381* (Cambridge, 1984), p. 67.

footnote, supplying bibliographical information as specified on pages 136–137.

We have divided the following information into two sections. Part A describes those rules which it is essential to master no matter what kind of essay you are writing (including examination answers). Part B sets out some of the more detailed conventions which govern the documentation of essays.

PART A: LAYOUT

Titles of texts

Titles of published books, plays (of any length), long poems, pamphlets and periodicals (including newspapers and magazines), works of classical literature, and films should be underlined: e.g. <u>David Copperfield</u> (novel), <u>Twelfth Night</u> (play), <u>Paradise Lost</u> (long poem), <u>Critical Quarterly</u> (periodical), Horace's <u>Ars Poetica</u> (Classical work), <u>Apocalypse Now</u> (film).

Notice how important it is to distinguish between titles and other names. <u>Hamlet</u> is the play; Hamlet the prince. <u>Wuthering Heights</u> is the novel; Wuthering Heights the house. Underlining is the equivalent in handwritten or typed manuscripts of printed italics. So what normally appears in this volume as *Othello* would be written as <u>Othello</u> in your essay.

Titles of articles, essays, short stories, short poems, songs, chapters of books, speeches, and newspaper articles are enclosed in quotation marks; e.g. 'The Flea' (short poem), 'The Prussian Officer' (short story), 'Middleton's Chess Strategies' (article), 'Thatcher Defects!' (newspaper headline).

Exceptions: Underlining titles or placing them within quotation marks does not apply to sacred writings (e.g. Bible, Koran, Old Testament, Gospels) or parts of a book (e.g. Preface, Introduction, Appendix).

It is generally incorrect to place quotation marks around a title of a published book which you have underlined. The exception is 'titles within titles', e.g. <u>'Vanity Fair': A Critical Study</u> (title of a book about *Vanity Fair*).

Quotations

Short verse quotations of a single line or part of a line should be incorporated within quotation marks as part of the running text of your essay. Quotations of two or three lines of verse are treated in the same way, with line endings indicated by a slash(/). For example:

1 In Julius Caesar, Antony says of Brutus, 'This was the noblest Roman of them all'.
2 The opening of Antony's famous funeral oration, 'Friends, Romans, Countrymen, lend me your ears;/ I come to bury Caesar not to praise him', is a carefully controlled piece of rhetoric.

Longer verse quotations of more than three lines should be indented from the main body of the text and introduced in most cases with a colon. Do not enclose indented quotations within quotation marks. For example:
It is worth pausing to consider the reasons Brutus gives to justify his decision to assassinate Caesar:

> It must be by his death; and for my part,
> I know no personal cause to spurn at him,
> But for the general. He would be crowned.
> How might that change his nature, there's the question.

At first glance his rationale may appear logical . . .

Prose quotations of less than three lines should be incorporated in the text of the essay, within quotation marks. Longer prose quotations should be indented and the quotation marks omitted. For example:

1 Before his downfall, Caesar rules with an iron hand. His political opponents, the Tribunes Marullus and Flavius, are 'put to silence' for the trivial offence of 'pulling scarfs off Caesar's image'.
2 It is interesting to note the rhetorical structure of Brutus's Forum speech:

> Romans, countrymen, and lovers, hear me for my cause, and be
> silent that you may hear. Believe me for my honour, and have
> respect to mine honour that you may believe. Censure me in
> your wisdom, and awake your senses, that you may the better
> judge.

Tenses: When you are relating the events that occur within a work of fiction or describing the author's technique, it is the convention to use the present tense. Even though Orwell published *Animal Farm* in 1945, the book *describes* the animals' seizure of Manor Farm. Similarly, Macbeth always *murders* Duncan, despite the passage of time.

PART B: DOCUMENTATION

When quoting from verse of more than twenty lines, provide line references: e.g. In 'Upon Appleton House' Marvell's mower moves 'With whistling scythe and elbow strong' (l.393).

Quotations from plays should be identified by act, scene and line references: e.g. Prospero, in Shakespeare's The Tempest, refers to Caliban as 'A devil, a born devil' (IV.1.188). (i.e. Act 4. Scene 1. Line 188).

Quotations from prose works should provide a chapter reference and, where appropriate, a page reference.

Bibliographies should list full details of all sources consulted. The way in which they are presented varies, but one standard format is as follows:

1 Books and articles are listed in alphabetical order by the author's last name. Initials are placed after the surname.
2 If you are referring to a chapter or article within a larger work, you list it by reference to the author of the article or chapter, not the editor (although the editor is also named in the reference).
3 Give (in parentheses) the place and date of publication, e.g. (London, 1962). These details can be found within the book itself. Here are some examples:

> Brockbank, J. P., 'Shakespeare's Histories, English and Roman', in Ricks, C. (ed.) English Drama to 1710 (Sphere History of Literature in the English Language) (London, 1971).
> Gurr, A., 'Richard III and the Democratic Process', Essays in Criticism 24 (1974), pp. 39–47.
> Spivack, B., Shakespeare and the Allegory of Evil (New York, 1958).

Footnotes: In general, try to avoid using footnotes and build your references into the body of the essay wherever possible. When you do use them give the full bibliographic reference to a work in the first instance and then use a short title: e.g. See K. Smidt, Unconformities in Shakespeare's History Plays (London, 1982), pp. 43–47 becomes Smidt (pp. 43–47) thereafter. Do not use terms such as 'ibid.' or 'op. cit.' unless you are absolutely sure of their meaning.

There is a principle behind all this seeming pedantry. The reader ought to be able to find and check your references and quotations as quickly and easily as possible. Give additional information, such as canto or volume number whenever you think it will assist your reader.

Works by Chaucer

The Riverside Chaucer (Oxford, 1988) is the standard volume containing Chaucer's complete works in their original Middle English form. Nevill Coghill's classic translation of *The Canterbury Tales* (Harmondsworth, 1951) is available as a Penguin paperback and remains an excellent quick introduction to the canon.

General introductory studies of Chaucer

Brewer, D, *An Introduction to Chaucer* (Harlow, 1984)

Hussey, M, Spearing, A C, Winny, J, *An Introduction to Chaucer* (Cambridge, 1965)

A study of the *General Prologue*

Cunningham, J, *The 'Prologue' to 'The Canterbury Tales': A Critical Study* (Harmondsworth, 1985): text and translation included

Longman Group UK Limited
*Longman House, Burnt Mill, Harlow, Essex, CM20 2JE, England
and Associated Companies throughout the World.*

First published 1989
ISBN 0 582 03790 5

*Set in 10/12 pt Century Schoolbook, Linotron 202
Printed in Great Britain by Bell and Bain LTD., Glasgow.*

Acknowledgements
We are grateful to the following for permission to reproduce copyright
material:

We are indebted to Houghton Mifflin Company for permission to reproduce extracts from *The Riverside Chaucer*, Third Edition, edited by
Larry D Benson. Copyright © 1987 by Houghton Mifflin Company.